COLLECTED POEMS

BY ROBERT GRAVES

Good-Bye to All That
The Real David Copperfield
I, Claudius
Claudius the God
The Antigua Stamp (Antigua, Penny, Puce)
Count Belisarius
Almost Forgotten Germany, *translation from German*
T. E. Lawrence to His Biographer
Sergeant Lamb's America (Sergeant Lamb of the Ninth)
With ALAN HODGE: The Reader Over Your Shoulder:
    A Handbook for Writers of English Prose
Proceed, Sergeant Lamb
With ALAN HODGE: The Long Week-End: A Social History of Britain, 1919–39
Wife to Mr. Milton
King Jesus
Hercules, My Shipmate (The Golden Fleece)
The White Goddess: A Historical Grammar of Poetic Myth
The Common Asphodel: Collected Essays on Poetry, 1922–49
The Islands of Unwisdom
Watch the North Wind Rise
The Golden Ass, *translation from Latin*
Occupation: Writer
With JOSHUA PODRO: The Nazarene Gospel Restored
Homer's Daughter
The Greek Myths
Cross and Sword, *translation from Spanish*
The Infant with the Globe, *translation from Spanish*
Adam's Rib
The Crowning Privilege
Winter in Majorca, *translation from French*
With JOSHUA PODRO: Jesus in Rome: A Conjecture
Lucan's 'Pharsalia,' *translation from Latin*
Suetonius's 'Twelve Caesars,' *translation from Latin*
English and Scottish Ballads
Collected Poems, 1955
They Hanged My Saintly Billy: The Life and Death of Dr. William Palmer
Good-Bye to All That, *new edition, revised*
5 Pens in Hand
The Anger of Achilles: Homer's *Iliad*, *translation from Greek*
Food for Centaurs
Greek Gods and Heroes
Collected Poems

ROBERT GRAVES

COLLECTED
POEMS

DOUBLEDAY & COMPANY, INC.
GARDEN CITY, NEW YORK

ACKNOWLEDGMENTS

The following poems appeared originally in *The New Yorker*: *Around the Mountain, Beauty in Trouble, The Blue-Fly, Cat-Goddesses, The Death Room, Here Live Your Life Out!, I'm Through with You For Ever, Joan and Darby, A Lost World, Lovers in Winter, My Name and I, The Naked and the Nude, Nightfall at Twenty Thousand Feet, A Slice of Wedding Cake, Twice of the Same Fever, The Twin of Sleep, '¡Wellcome, to the Caves of Artá!', Woman and Tree*.

Acknowledgment is also made to *Hudson Review, Poetry, Good Housekeeping, The Atlantic Monthly, Tomorrow, Time and Tide*, the New York Times, *Saturday Review, Harper's Magazine*, and to Farrar, Straus & Cudahy, Inc., for the poems which originally appeared in *Collected Poems 1934–1945* by Robert Graves (copyright 1946 by International Authors N.V.).

TO CALLIOPE

Permit me here a simple brief aside,
    Calliope,
You who have shown such patience with my pride
    And obstinacy:

Am I not loyal to you? I say no less
    Than is to say;
If more, only from angry-heartedness,
    Not for display.

But you know, I know, and you know I know
    My principal curse:
Shame at the mounting dues I have come to owe
    A devil of verse,

Who caught me young, ingenuous and uncouth,
    Prompting me how
To evade the patent clumsiness of truth—
    Which I do now.

No: nothing reads so fresh as I first thought,
    Or as you could wish—
Yet must I, when far worse is eagerly bought,
    Cry stinking fish?

FOREWORD

These poems follow a roughly chronological order. The first was written in the summer of 1914, and shows where I stood at the age of nineteen before getting caught up by the First World War, which permanently changed my outlook on life.

Sixteen years of the forty-seven that have since elapsed were spent in England; twenty-one in Spain—which has become my permanent home—most of the rest in Wales, France, Egypt, Switzerland, and the United States. But somehow these poems have never adopted a foreign accent or colouring; they remain true to the Anglo-Irish poetic tradition into which I was born.

I published four successive collections in 1926, 1938, 1947, and 1955, and on each occasion suppressed all poems that no longer passed muster. I now do the same again, with the result that this new collection is not very much larger than *Collected Poems, 1926*. Critics may decide that benefit of the doubt is being too generously conceded. They will be right, of course. At any rate, I can promise that no silver spoons have been thrown out with the refuse, and that I have been fair to my younger, middle, and elder selves.

Deyá   R.G.
Majorca

CONTENTS

I

II

III

IV

V

VI

VII

X

XI

XII

I

IN THE WILDERNESS

He, of his gentleness,
Thirsting and hungering
Walked in the wilderness;
Soft words of grace he spoke
Unto lost desert-folk
That listened wondering.
He heard the bittern call
From ruined palace-wall,
Answered him brotherly;
He held communion
With the she-pelican
Of lonely piety.
Basilisk, cockatrice,
Flocked to his homilies,
With mail of dread device,
With monstrous barbèd stings,
With eager dragon-eyes;
Great bats on leathern wings
And old, blind, broken things
Mean in their miseries.
Then ever with him went,
Of all his wanderings
Comrade, with ragged coat,
Gaunt ribs—poor innocent—
Bleeding foot, burning throat,
The guileless young scapegoat:
For forty nights and days
Followed in Jesus' ways,
Sure guard behind him kept,
Tears like a lover wept.

THE HAUNTED HOUSE

'Come, surly fellow, come: a song!'
   What, fools? Sing to you?
Choose from the clouded tales of wrong
   And terror I bring to you:

Of a night so torn with cries,
   Honest men sleeping
Start awake with rabid eyes,
   Bone-chilled, flesh creeping,

Of spirits in the web-hung room
   Up above the stable,
Groans, knockings in the gloom,
   The dancing table,

Of demons in the dry well
   That cheep and mutter,
Clanging of an unseen bell,
   Blood choking the gutter,

Of lust frightful, past belief,
   Lurking unforgotten,
Unrestrainable endless grief
   In breasts long rotten.

A song? What laughter or what song
   Can this house remember?
Do flowers and butterflies belong
   To a blind December?

REPROACH

Your grieving moonlight face looks down
   Through the forest of my fears,
Crowned with a spiny bramble-crown,
   Bedewed with evening tears.

Why do you say 'untrue, unkind',
   Reproachful eyes that vex my sleep?
Straining in memory, I can find
   No cause why you should weep.

Untrue? But when, what broken oath?
   Unkind? I know not even your name.
Unkind, untrue, you brand me both,
   Scalding my heart with shame.

The black trees shudder, dropping snow,
   The stars tumble and spin.
Speak, speak, or how may a child know
   His ancestral sin?

THE FINDING OF LOVE

Pale at first and cold,
Like wizard's lily-bloom
Conjured from the gloom,
Like torch of glow-worm seen
Through grasses shining green
By children half in fright,
Or Christmas candlelight
Flung on the outer snow,
Or tinsel stars that show
Their evening glory
With sheen of fairy story—

Now with his blaze
Love dries the cobweb maze
Dew-sagged upon the corn,
He brings the flowering thorn,
Mayfly and butterfly,
And pigeons in the sky,
Robin and thrush,
And the long bulrush,
Bird-cherry under the leaf,
Earth in a silken dress,
With end to grief,
With joy in steadfastness.

'THE GENERAL ELIOTT'

He fell in victory's fierce pursuit,
   Holed through and through with shot;
A sabre sweep had hacked him deep
   'Twixt neck and shoulder-knot.

The potman cannot well recall,
   The ostler never knew,
Whether that day was Malplaquet,
   The Boyne, or Waterloo.

But there he hangs, a tavern sign,
   With foolish bold regard
For cock and hen and loitering men
   And wagons down the yard.

Raised high above the hayseed world
   He smokes his china pipe;
And now surveys the orchard ways,
   The damsons clustering ripe—

Stares at the churchyard slabs beyond,
   Where country neighbours lie:
Their brief renown set lowly down,
   But his invades the sky.

He grips a tankard of brown ale
   That spills a generous foam:
Often he drinks, they say, and winks
   At drunk men lurching home.

No upstart hero may usurp
   That honoured swinging seat;
His seasons pass with pipe and glass
   Until the tale's complete—

And paint shall keep his buttons bright
   Though all the world's forgot
Whether he died for England's pride
   By battle or by pot.

ROCKY ACRES

This is a wild land, country of my choice,
With harsh craggy mountain, moor ample and bare.
Seldom in these acres is heard any voice
But voice of cold water that runs here and there
Through rocks and lank heather growing without care.
No mice in the heath run, no song-birds fly
For fear of the buzzard that floats in the sky.

He soars and he hovers, rocking on his wings,
He scans his wide parish with a sharp eye,
He catches the trembling of small hidden things,
He tears them in pieces, dropping them from the sky;
Tenderness and pity the heart will deny,
Where life is but nourished by water and rock—
A hardy adventure, full of fear and shock.

Time has never journeyed to this lost land,
Crakeberry and heather bloom out of date,
The rocks jut, the streams flow singing on either hand,
Careless if the season be early or late,
The skies wander overhead, now blue, now slate;
Winter would be known by his cutting snow
If June did not borrow his armour also.

Yet this is my country, beloved by me best,
The first land that rose from Chaos and the Flood,
Nursing no valleys for comfort or rest,
Trampled by no shod hooves, bought with no blood.
Sempiternal country whose barrows have stood
Stronghold for demigods when on earth they go,
Terror for fat burghers on far plains below.

OUTLAWS

Owls—they whinny down the night;
  Bats go zigzag by.
Ambushed in shadow beyond sight
  The outlaws lie.

Old gods, tamed to silence, there
  In the wet woods they lurk,
Greedy of human stuff to snare
  In nets of murk.

Look up, else your eye will drown
  In a moving sea of black;
Between the tree-tops, upside down,
  Goes the sky-track.

Look up, else your feet will stray
  Into that ambuscade
Where spider-like they trap their prey
  With webs of shade.

For though creeds whirl away in dust,
  Faith dies and men forget,
These agèd gods of power and lust
  Cling to life yet—

Old gods almost dead, malign,
  Starving for unpaid dues:
Incense and fire, salt, blood and wine
  And a drumming muse,

Banished to woods and a sickly moon,
  Shrunk to mere bogey things,
Who spoke with thunder once at noon
  To prostrate kings:

With thunder from an open sky
   To warrior, virgin, priest,
Bowing in fear with a dazzled eye
   Toward the dread East—

Proud gods, humbled, sunk so low,
   Living with ghosts and ghouls,
And ghosts of ghosts and last year's snow
   And dead toadstools.

ONE HARD LOOK

Small gnats that fly
In hot July
And lodge in sleeping ears
Can rouse therein
A trumpet's din
With Day of Judgement fears.

Small mice at night
Can wake more fright
Than lions at midday;
A straw will crack
The camel's back—
There is no easier way.

One smile relieves
A heart that grieves
Though deadly sad it be,
And one hard look
Can close the book
That lovers love to see.

A FROSTY NIGHT

'Alice, dear, what ails you,
  Dazed and lost and shaken?
Has the chill night numbed you?
  Is it fright you have taken?'

'Mother, I am very well,
  I was never better.
Mother, do not hold me so,
  Let me write my letter.'

'Sweet, my dear, what ails you?'
  'No, but I am well.
The night was cold and frosty—
  There's no more to tell.'

'Ay, the night was frosty,
  Coldly gaped the moon,
Yet the birds seemed twittering
  Through green boughs of June.

'Soft and thick the snow lay,
  Stars danced in the sky—
Not all the lambs of May-day
  Skip so bold and high.

'Your feet were dancing, Alice,
  Seemed to dance on air,
You looked a ghost or angel
  In the star-light there.

'Your eyes were frosted star-light;
  Your heart, fire and snow.
Who was it said, "I love you"?'
  'Mother, let me go!'

ALLIE

Allie, call the birds in,
  The birds from the sky!
Allie calls, Allie sings,
  Down they all fly:
First there came
Two white doves,
  Then a sparrow from his nest,
Then a clucking bantam hen,
  Then a robin red-breast.

Allie, call the beasts in,
  The beasts, every one!
Allie calls, Allie sings,
  In they all run:
First there came
Two black lambs,
  Then a grunting Berkshire sow,
Then a dog without a tail,
  Then a red and white cow.

Allie, call the fish up,
  The fish from the stream!
Allie calls, Allie sings,
  Up they all swim:
First there came
Two gold fish,
  A minnow and a miller's thumb,
Then a school of little trout,
  Then the twisting eels come.

Allie, call the children,
  Call them from the green!
Allie calls, Allie sings,
  Soon they run in:
First there came
Tom and Madge,
  Kate and I who'll not forget
How we played by the water's edge
  Till the April sun set.

UNICORN AND THE WHITE DOE

Unicorn with bursting heart
  Breath of love has drawn:
On his desolate crags apart,
  At rumour of dawn,

Has blared aloud his pride
  This long age mute,
Lurched his horn from side to side,
  Lunged with his foot.

'Like a storm of sand I run
  Breaking the desert's boundaries,
I go in hiding from the sun
  In thick shade of trees.

'Straight was the track I took
  Across the plains, but here with briar
And mire the tangled alleys crook,
  Baulking desire.

'O there, what glinted white?
  (A bough still shakes.)
What was it darted from my sight
  Through the forest brakes?

'Where are you fled from me?
  I pursue, you fade;
I run, you hide from me
  In the dark glade.

'Towering high the trees grow,
  The grass grows thick.
Where you are I do not know,
  You run so quick.'

HENRY AND MARY

Henry was a young king,
    Mary was his queen;
He gave her a snowdrop
    On a stalk of green.

Then all for his kindness
    And all for his care
She gave him a new-laid egg
    In the garden there.

'Love, can you sing?'
               'I cannot sing.'
  'Or tell a tale?'
              'Not one I know.'
'Then let us play at queen and king
    As down the garden walks we go.'

LOVE WITHOUT HOPE

Love without hope, as when the young bird-catcher
Swept off his tall hat to the Squire's own daughter,
So let the imprisoned larks escape and fly
Singing about her head, as she rode by.

WHAT DID I DREAM?

What did I dream? I do not know—
  The fragments fly like chaff.
Yet, strange, my mind was tickled so
  I cannot help but laugh.

Pull the curtains close again,
  Tuck me grandly in;
Must a world of humour wane
  Because birds begin

Complaining in a fretful tone,
  Rousing me from sleep—
The finest entertainment known,
  And given rag-cheap?

THE COUNTRY DANCE

More slowly the sun travels West,
   Earth warming beneath,
Man's heart swelling tight in his breast
   As a bud in the sheath.

For the tender and unquiet season,
   The Spring, drawing on
Kindles flame in the eye, chokes the reason
   And silvers the swan.

Leap high, jealous Ralph; jet it neat,
   Merry Jill, and remove
By employment of elbows and feet
   The green sickness of love.

THE TROLL'S NOSEGAY

A simple nosegay! was that much to ask?
(Winter still nagged, with scarce a bud yet showing.)
He loved her ill, if he resigned the task.
'Somewhere,' she cried, 'there must be blossom blowing.'
It seems my lady wept and the troll swore
By Heaven he hated tears: he'd cure her spleen—
Where she had begged one flower he'd shower fourscore,
A bunch fit to amaze a China Queen.

Cold fog-drawn Lily, pale mist-magic Rose
He conjured, and in a glassy cauldron set
With elvish unsubstantial Mignonette
And such vague bloom as wandering dreams enclose.
But she?
   Awed,
     Charmed to tears,
         Distracted,
           Yet—
Even yet, perhaps, a trifle piqued—who knows?

THE HILLS OF MAY

Walking with a virgin heart
   The green hills of May,
Me, the Wind, she took as lover
   By her side to play,

Let me toss her untied hair,
   Let me shake her gown,
Careless though the daisies redden,
   Though the sun frown,

Scorning in her gay habit
   Lesser love than this,
My cool spiritual embracing,
   My secret kiss.

So she walked, the proud lady,
   So danced or ran,
So she loved with a whole heart,
   Neglecting man . . .

Fade, fail, innocent stars
   On the green of May:
She has left our bournes for ever,
   Too fine to stay.

LOST LOVE

His eyes are quickened so with grief,
He can watch a grass or leaf
Every instant grow; he can
Clearly through a flint wall see,
Or watch the startled spirit flee
From the throat of a dead man.
   Across two counties he can hear
And catch your words before you speak.
The woodlouse or the maggot's weak
Clamour rings in his sad ear,
And noise so slight it would surpass
Credence—drinking sound of grass,
Worm talk, clashing jaws of moth
Chumbling holes in cloth;
The groan of ants who undertake
Gigantic loads for honour's sake
(Their sinews creak, their breath comes thin);
Whir of spiders when they spin,
And minute whispering, mumbling, sighs
Of idle grubs and flies.
   This man is quickened so with grief,
He wanders god-like or like thief
Inside and out, below, above,
Without relief seeking lost love.

VAIN AND CARELESS

Lady, lovely lady,
  Careless and gay!
Once, when a beggar called,
  She gave her child away.

The beggar took the baby,
  Wrapped it in a shawl—
'Bring him back,' the lady said,
  'Next time you call.'

Hard by lived a vain man,
  So vain and so proud
He would walk on stilts
  To be seen by the crowd,

Up above the chimney pots,
  Tall as a mast—
And all the people ran about
  Shouting till he passed.

'A splendid match surely,'
  Neighbours saw it plain,
'Although she is so careless,
  Although he is so vain.'

But the lady played bobcherry,
  Did not see or care,
As the vain man went by her,
  Aloft in the air.

This gentle-born couple
  Lived and died apart—
Water will not mix with oil,
  Nor vain with careless heart.

AN ENGLISH WOOD

This valley wood is pledged
To the set shape of things,
And reasonably hedged:
Here are no harpies fledged,
No rocs may clap their wings,
Nor gryphons wave their stings.
Here, poised in quietude,
Calm elementals brood
On the set shape of things:
They fend away alarms
From this green wood.
Here nothing is that harms—
No bulls with lungs of brass,
No toothed or spiny grass,
No tree whose clutching arms
Drink blood when travellers pass,
No mount of glass;
No bardic tongues unfold
Satires or charms.
Only, the lawns are soft,
The tree-stems, grave and old;
Slow branches sway aloft,
The evening air comes cold,
The sunset scatters gold.
Small grasses toss and bend,
Small pathways idly tend
Towards no fearful end.

THE BEDPOST

Sleepy Betsy from her pillow
   Sees the post and ball
Of her sister's wooden bedstead
   Shadowed on the wall.

Now this grave young warrior standing
   With uncovered head
Tells her stories of old battle
   As she lies in bed:

How the Emperor and the Farmer,
   Fighting knee to knee,
Broke their swords but whirled their scabbards
   Till they gained the sea.

How the ruler of that shore
   Foully broke his oath,
Gave them beds in his sea cave,
   Then stabbed them both.

How the daughters of the Emperor,
   Diving boldly through,
Caught and killed their father's murderer
   Old Cro-bar-cru.

How the Farmer's sturdy sons
   Fought the Giant Gog,
Threw him into Stony Cataract
   In the land of Og.

Will and Abel were their names,
   Though they went by others:
He could tell ten thousand stories
   Of these lusty brothers.

How the Emperor's elder daughter
    Fell in love with Will
And went with him to the Court of Venus
    Over Hoo Hill;

How Gog's wife encountered Abel
    Whom she hated most,
Stole away his arms and helmet,
    Turned him to a post.

As a post he shall stay rooted
    For yet many years,
Until a maiden shall release him
    With pitying tears.

But Betsy likes the bloodier stories,
    Clang and clash of fight,
And Abel wanes with the spent candle—
    'Sweetheart, good-night!'

THE PIER-GLASS

Lost manor where I walk continually
A ghost, though yet in woman's flesh and blood.
Up your broad stairs mounting with outspread fingers
And gliding steadfast down your corridors
I come by nightly custom to this room,
And even on sultry afternoons I come
Drawn by a thread of time-sunk memory.

Empty, unless for a huge bed of state
Shrouded with rusty curtains drooped awry.
(A puppet theatre where malignant fancy
Peoples the wings with fear.) At my right hand
A ravelled bell-pull hangs in readiness
To summon me from attic glooms above
Service of elder ghosts; here, at my left,
A sullen pier-glass, cracked from side to side,
Scorns to present the face (as do new mirrors)
With a lying flush, but shows it melancholy
And pale, as faces grow that look in mirrors.

Is there no life, nothing but the thin shadow
And blank foreboding, never a wainscot rat
Rasping a crust? Or at the window-pane
No fly, no bluebottle, no starveling spider?
The windows frame a prospect of cold skies
Half-merged with sea, as at the first creation—
Abstract, confusing welter. Face about,
Peer rather in the glass once more, take note
Of self, the grey lips and long hair dishevelled,
Sleep-staring eyes. Ah, mirror, for Christ's love
Give me one token that there still abides
Remote—beyond this island mystery,
So be it only this side Hope, somewhere,
In streams, on sun-warm mountain pasturage—
True life, natural breath; not this phantasma.

APPLES AND WATER

Dust in a cloud, blinding weather,
    Drums that rattle and roar!
A mother and daughter stood together
    By their cottage door.

'Mother, the heavens are bright like brass,
    The dust is shaken high,
With labouring breath the soldiers pass,
    Their lips are cracked and dry.

'Mother, I'll throw them apples down,
    I'll fetch them cups of water.'
The mother turned with an angry frown,
    Holding back her daughter.

'But, mother, see, they faint with thirst,
    They march away to war.'
'Ay, daughter, these are not the first
    And there will come yet more.

'There is no water can supply them
    In western streams that flow;
There is no fruit can satisfy them
    On orchard-trees that grow.

'Once in my youth I gave, poor fool,
    A soldier apples and water;
And may I die before you cool
    Such drouth as his, my daughter.'

ANGRY SAMSON

Are they blind, the lords of Gaza
   In their strong towers,
Who declare Samson pillow-smothered
   And stripped of his powers?

O stolid Philistines,
   Stare now in amaze
At my foxes running in your cornfields
   With their tails ablaze,

At swung jaw-bone, at bees swarming
   In the stark lion's hide,
At these, the gates of well-walled Gaza
   A-clank to my stride.

DOWN

Downstairs a clock had chimed, two o'clock only.
Then outside from the hen-roost crowing came.
Why should the shift-wing call against the clock,
Three hours from dawn? Now shutters click and knock,
And he remembers a sad superstition
Unfitting for the sick-bed . . . Turn aside,
Distract, divide, ponder the simple tales
That puzzled childhood; riddles, turn them over—
Half-riddles, answerless, the more intense.
Lost bars of music tinkling with no sense
Recur, drowning uneasy superstition.

Mouth open, he was lying, this sick man,
And sinking all the while; how had he come
To sink? On better nights his dream went flying,
Dipping, sailing the pasture of his sleep,
But now (since clock and cock) had sunk him down
Through mattress, bed, floor, floors beneath, stairs, cellars,
Through deep foundations of the manse; still sinking
Through unturned earth. How had he magicked space
With inadvertent motion or word uttered
Of too-close-packed intelligence (such there are),
That he should penetrate with sliding ease
Dense earth, compound of ages, granite ribs
And groins? Consider: there was some word uttered,
Some abracadabra—then, like a stage-ghost,
Funereally with weeping, down, drowned, lost!
Oh, to be a child once more, sprawling at ease
On smooth turf of a ruined castle court!
Once he had dropped a stone between the slabs
That masked an ancient well, mysteriously
Plunging his mind down with it. Hear it go
Rattling and rocketing into secret void!
Count slowly: one, two three! and echoes come
Fainter and fainter, merged in the general hum
Of bees and flies; only a thin draught rises
To chill the drowsy air. There he had lain

As if unborn, until life floated back
From the deep waters.

                  Oh, to renew now
That bliss of repossession, kindly sun
Forfeit for ever, and the towering sky!

Falling, falling! Day closed up behind him.
Now stunned by the violent subterrene flow
Of rivers, whirling down to hiss below
On the flame-axis of this terrible earth;
Toppling upon their waterfall, O spirit . . .

MERMAID, DRAGON, FIEND

In my childhood rumours ran
　　Of a world beyond our door—
Terrors to the life of man
　　That the highroad held in store.

Of the mermaids' doleful game
　　In deep water I heard tell,
Of lofty dragons belching flame,
　　Of the hornèd fiend of Hell.

Tales like these were too absurd
　　For my laughter-loving ear:
Soon I mocked at all I heard,
　　Though with cause indeed for fear.

Now I know the mermaid kin
　　I find them bound by natural laws:
They have neither tail nor fin,
　　But are deadlier for that cause.

Dragons have no darting tongues,
　　Teeth saw-edged, nor rattling scales;
No fire issues from their lungs,
　　No black poison from their tails:

For they are creatures of dark air,
　　Unsubstantial tossing forms,
Thunderclaps of man's despair
　　In mid-whirl of mental storms.

And there's a true and only fiend
　　Worse than prophets prophesy,
Whose full powers to hurt are screened
　　Lest the race of man should die.

Ever in vain will courage plot
   The dragon's death, in coat of proof;
Or love abjure the mermaid grot;
   Or faith denounce the cloven hoof.

Mermaids will not be denied
   The last bubbles of our shame,
The dragon flaunts an unpierced hide,
   The true fiend governs in God's name.

II

IN PROCESSION

Often, half-way to sleep,
Not yet sunken deep—
The sudden moment on me comes
From a mountain shagged and steep,
With terrible roll of dream drums,
Reverberations, cymbals, horns replying.
When with standards flying,
Horsemen in clouds behind,
The coloured pomps unwind,
Carnival wagons
With their saints and their dragons
On the scroll of my teeming mind:
The Creation and Flood
With our Saviour's Blood
And fat Silenus' flagons,
And every rare beast
From the South and East,
Both greatest and least,
On and on,
In endless, variant procession.
I stand at the top rungs
Of a ladder reared in the air,
And I rail in strange tongues,
So the crowds murmur and stare;
Then volleys again the blare
Of horns, and summer flowers
Fly scattering in showers,
And the sun leaps in the sky,
While the drums thumping by
Proclaim me . . .

Oh, then, when I wake,
Could I courage take
To renew my speech,
Could I stretch and reach
The flowers and the ripe fruit
Laid out at the ladder's foot,
Could I rip a silken shred

From the banner tossed ahead,
Could I call a double-flam
From the drums, could the goat
Horned with gold, could the ram
With a flank like a barn-door,
The dwarf, the blackamoor,
Could Jonah and the Whale
And the Holy Grail,
The Ape with his platter
Going clitter-clatter,
The Nymphs and the Satyr,
And every marvellous matter
Come before me here,
Standing near and clear—
Could I make it so that you
Might wonder at them too!
—Glories of land and sea,
Of Heaven glittering free,
Castles hugely built in Spain,
Glories of Cockaigne,
Of that spicy kingdom, Cand,
Of the Delectable Land,
Of the Land of Crooked Stiles,
Of the Fortunate Isles,
Of the more than three-score miles
That to Babylon lead
(A pretty city indeed
Built on a four-square plan),
Of the Land of the Gold Man
Whose eager horses whinny
In their cribs of gold,
Of the Land of Whipperginny,
Of the land where none grows old . . .

But cowardly I tell,
Rather, of the Town of Hell—
A huddle of dirty woes
And houses in fading rows

Straggled through space:
Hell has no market-place,
Nor point where four ways meet,
Nor principal street,
Nor barracks, nor Town Hall,
Nor shops at all,
Nor rest for weary feet,
Nor theatre, square, or park,
Nor lights after dark,
Nor churches, nor inns,
Nor convenience for sins—
Neither ends nor begins,
Rambling, limitless, hated well,
This Town of Hell
Where between sleep and sleep I dwell.

WARNING TO CHILDREN

Children, if you dare to think
Of the greatness, rareness, muchness,
Fewness of this precious only
Endless world in which you say
You live, you think of things like this:
Blocks of slate enclosing dappled
Red and green, enclosing tawny
Yellow nets, enclosing white
And black acres of dominoes,
Where a neat brown paper parcel
Tempts you to untie the string.
In the parcel a small island,
On the island a large tree,
On the tree a husky fruit.
Strip the husk and pare the rind off:
In the kernel you will see
Blocks of slate enclosed by dappled
Red and green, enclosed by tawny
Yellow nets, enclosed by white
And black acres of dominoes,
Where the same brown paper parcel—
Children, leave the string alone!
For who dares undo the parcel
Finds himself at once inside it,
On the island, in the fruit,
Blocks of slate about his head,
Finds himself enclosed by dappled
Green and red, enclosed by yellow
Tawny nets, enclosed by black
And white acres of dominoes,
With the same brown paper parcel
Still untied upon his knee.
And, if he then should dare to think
Of the fewness, muchness, rareness,
Greatness of this endless only
Precious world in which he says
He lives—he then unties the string.

ALICE

When that prime heroine of our nation, Alice,
Climbing courageously in through the Palace
Of Looking Glass, found it inhabited
By chessboard personages, white and red,
Involved in never-ending tournament,
She being of a speculative bent
Had long foreshadowed something of the kind,
Asking herself: 'Suppose I stood behind
And viewed the fireplace of Their drawing-room
From hearthrug level, why must I assume
That what I'd see would need to correspond
With what I now see? And the rooms beyond?'

Proved right, yet not content with what she had done,
Alice decided to increase her fun:
She set herself, with truly British pride
In being a pawn and playing for her side,
And simple faith in simple stratagem,
To learn the rules and moves and perfect them.
So prosperously there she settled down
That six moves only and she'd won her crown—
A triumph surely! But her greater feat
Was rounding these adventures off complete:
Accepting them, when safe returned again,
As queer but true—not only in the main
True, but as true as anything you'd swear to,
The usual three dimensions you are heir to.
For Alice, though a child, could understand
That neither did this chance-discovered land
Make nohow or contrariwise the clean
Dull round of mid-Victorian routine,
Nor did Victoria's golden rule extend
Beyond the glass: it came to the dead end
Where empty hearses turn about; thereafter
Begins that lubberland of dream and laughter,
The red-and-white-flower-spangled hedge, the grass
Where Apuleius pastured his Gold Ass,
Where young Gargantua made whole holiday . . .

But farther from our heroine not to stray,
Let us observe with what uncommon sense—
Though a secure and easy reference
Between Red Queen and Kitten could be found—
She made no false assumption on that ground
(A trap in which the scientist would fall)
That queens and kittens are identical.

RICHARD ROE AND JOHN DOE

Richard Roe wished himself Solomon,
Made cuckold, you should know, by one John Doe:
Solomon's neck was firm enough to bear
Some score of antlers more than Roe could wear.

Richard Roe wished himself Alexander,
Being robbed of house and land by the same hand:
Ten thousand acres or a principal town
Would have cost Alexander scarce a frown.

Richard Roe wished himself Job the prophet,
Sunk past reclaim in stinking rags and shame—
However ill Job's plight, his own was worse:
He knew no God to call on or to curse.

He wished himself Job, Solomon, Alexander,
For patience, wisdom, power to overthrow
Misfortune; but with spirit so unmanned
That most of all he wished himself John Doe.

THE WITCHES' CAULDRON

In sudden cloud that, blotting distance out,
Confused the compass of the traveller's mind,
Biased his course: three times from the hill's crest
Trying to descend but with no track to follow,
Nor visible landmark—three times he had struck
The same sedged pool of steaming desolation,
The same black monolith rearing up before it.
This third time then he stood and recognized
The Witches' Cauldron, only known before
By hearsay, fly-like on whose rim he had crawled
Three times and three times dipped to climb again
Its uncouth sides, so to go crawling on.

By falls of scree, moss-mantled slippery rock,
Wet bracken, drunken gurgling watercourses
He escaped, limping, at last, and broke the circuit—
Travelling down and down; but smooth descent
Interrupted by new lakes and ridges,
Sprawling unmortared walls of boulder granite,
Marshes; one arm hung bruised where he had fallen;
Blood in a sticky trickle smeared his cheek;
Sweat, gathering at his eyebrows, ran full beads
Into his eyes, which made them smart and blur.

At last he blundered on some shepherd's hut—
He thought, the hut took pity and appeared—
With mounds of peat and welcome track of wheels
Which he now followed to a broad green road
That ran from right to left; but still at fault,
The mist being still on all, with little pause
He chose the easier way, the downward way.

Legs were dog-tired already, but this road,
Gentle descent with some relief of guidance,
Maintained his shambling five miles to the hour
Coloured with day-dreams. Then a finger-post
Moved through the mist, pointing into his face,
Yet when he stopped to read gave him no comfort.

Seventeen miles to—somewhere, God knows where—
The paint was weathered to a puzzle
Which cold-unfocused eyes could not attempt—
And jerking a derisive thumb behind it
Up a rough stream-wet path: 'The Witches' Cauldron,
One mile.' Only a mile
For two good hours of stumbling steeplechase!
There was a dead snake by some humorous hand
Twined on the pointing finger; far away
A bull roared hoarsely, but all else was mist.

Then anger overcame him . . .

ANCESTORS

My New Year's drink is mulled to-night
  And hot sweet vapours roofward twine.
The shades cry *Gloria!* with delight
  As down they troop to taste old wine.

They crowd about the crackling fire,
  Impatient as the rites begin;
Mulled porto is their souls' desire—
  Porto well aged with nutmeg in.

'Ha,' cries the first, 'my Alma wine
  Of one-and-seventy years ago!'
The second cheers 'God bless the vine!'
  The third and fourth like cockerels crow:

They crow and clap their arms for wings,
  They have small pride or breeding left—
Two grey-beards, a tall youth who sings,
  A soldier with his cheek-bone cleft.

O *Gloria!* for each ghostly shape,
  That whiffled like a candle smoke,
Now fixed and ruddy with the grape
  And mirrored at the polished oak.

I watch their brightening boastful eyes,
  I hear the toast their glasses clink:
'May this young man in drink grown wise
  Die, as we also died, in drink!'

Their reedy voices I abhor,
  I am alive at least, and young.
I dash their swill upon the floor:
  Let them lap grovelling, tongue to tongue.

THE CORONATION MURDER

Old Becker crawling in the night
  From his grave at the stair-foot,
Labours up the long flight,
  Feeble, dribbling, black as soot,
Quakes at his own ghostly fright.

A cat goes past with lantern eyes,
  Shooting splendour through the dark.
'Murder! Help!' a voice cries
  In nightmare; the son dreams that stark
In lead his vanished father lies.

A stair-top glimmer points the goal.
  Becker goes wavering up, tongue-tied,
Stoops, with eye to keyhole . . .
  There, a tall candle by her side,
Delilah sits, serene and whole.

Her fingers turn the prayer-book leaves,
  Her features hint no mental strife:
Soft and calm her breast heaves:
  Thus calmly with his cobbling knife
She stabbed him through; now never grieves.

Baffled, aghast with hate, mouse-poor,
  He glares and clatters the brass knob.
Through his heart it slid sure:
  He bowed, he fell with never a sob.
Again she stabbed, now sits secure,

Praying (as she has always prayed)
  For great Victoria's Majesty,
Droning prayer for God's aid
  To succour long dead Royalty,
The Consort Prince, Queen Adelaide . . .

She falls asleep, the clocks chime two;
  Old Becker sinks to unquiet rest.
Loud and sad the cats mew.
  Lead weighs cruelly on his breast,
His bones are tufted with mildew.

CHILDREN OF DARKNESS

We spurred our parents to the kiss,
Though doubtfully they shrank from this—
Day had no courage to pursue
What lusty dark alone might do:
Then were we joined from their caress
In heat of midnight, one from two.

This night-seed knew no discontent:
In certitude our changings went.
Though there were veils about his face,
With forethought, even in that pent place,
Down toward the light his way we bent
To kingdoms of more ample space.

Is Day prime error, that regret
For Darkness roars unstifled yet?
That in this freedom, by faith won,
Only acts of doubt are done?
That unveiled eyes with tears are wet—
We loathe to gaze upon the sun?

THE COOL WEB

Children are dumb to say how hot the day is,
How hot the scent is of the summer rose,
How dreadful the black wastes of evening sky,
How dreadful the tall soldiers drumming by.

But we have speech, to chill the angry day,
And speech, to dull the rose's cruel scent.
We spell away the overhanging night,
We spell away the soldiers and the fright.

There's a cool web of language winds us in,
Retreat from too much joy or too much fear:
We grow sea-green at last and coldly die
In brininess and volubility.

But if we let our tongues lose self-possession,
Throwing off language and its watery clasp
Before our death, instead of when death comes,
Facing the wide glare of the children's day,
Facing the rose, the dark sky and the drums,
We shall go mad no doubt and die that way.

LOVE IN BARRENNESS

Below the ridge a raven flew
And we heard the lost curlew
Mourning out of sight below.
Mountain tops were touched with snow;
Even the long dividing plain
Showed no wealth of sheep or grain,
But fields of boulders lay like corn
And raven's croak was shepherd's horn
Where slow cloud-shadow strayed across
A pasture of thin heath and moss.

The North Wind rose: I saw him press
With lusty force against your dress,
Moulding your body's inward grace
And streaming off from your set face;
So now no longer flesh and blood
But poised in marble flight you stood.
O wingless Victory, loved of men,
Who could withstand your beauty then?

SONG OF CONTRARIETY

Far away is close at hand,
Close joined is far away,
Love shall come at your command
Yet will not stay.

At summons of your dream-despair
She might not disobey,
But slid close down beside you there,
And complaisant lay.

Yet now her flesh and blood consent
In the hours of day,
Joy and passion both are spent,
Twining clean away.

Is the person empty air,
Is the spectre clay,
That love, lent substance by despair,
Wanes and leaves you lonely there
On the bridal day?

THE PRESENCE

Why say 'death'? Death is neither harsh nor kind:
Other pleasures or pains could hold the mind
If she were dead. For dead is gone indeed,
Lost beyond recovery and need,
Discarded, ended, rotted underground—
Of whom no personal feature could be found
To stand out from the soft blur evenly spread
On memory, if she were truly dead.

But living still, barred from accustomed use
Of body and dress and motion, with profuse
Reproaches (since this anguish of her grew
Do I still love her as I swear I do?)
She fills the house and garden terribly
With her bewilderment, accusing me,
Till every stone and flower, table and book,
Cries out her name, pierces me with her look,
'You are deaf, listen!
You are blind, see!'
                How deaf or blind,
When horror of the grave maddens the mind
With those same pangs that lately choked her breath,
Altered her substance, and made sport of death?

THE LAND OF WHIPPERGINNY

Come closer yet, my honeysuckle, my sweetheart Jinny:
    A low sun is gilding the bloom of the wood—
Is it Heaven, or Hell, or the Land of Whipperginny
    That holds this fairy lustre, not yet understood?

For stern proud psalms from the chapel on the moors
    Waver in the night wind, their firm rhythm broken,
Lugubriously twisted to a howling of whores
    Or lent an airy glory too strange to be spoken.

Soon the risen Moon will peer down with pity,
    Drawing us in secret by an ivory gate
To the fruit-plats and fountains of her silver city
    Where lovers need not argue the tokens of fate.

IN NO DIRECTION

To go in no direction
   Surely as carelessly,
Walking on the hills alone,
   I never found easy.

Either I sent leaf or stick
   Twirling in the air,
Whose fall might be prophetic,
   Pointing 'there',

Or in superstition
   Edged somewhat away
From a sure direction,
   Yet could not stray,

Or undertook the climb
   That I had avoided
Directionless some other time,
   Or had not avoided,

Or called as companion
   Some eyeless ghost
And held his no direction
   Till my feet were lost.

THE CASTLE

Walls, mounds, enclosing corrugations
Of darkness, moonlight on dry grass.
Walking this courtyard, sleepless, in fever;
Planning to use—but by definition
There's no way out, no way out—
Rope-ladders, baulks of timber, pulleys,
A rocket whizzing over the walls and moat—
Machines easy to improvise.
                                        No escape,
No such thing; to dream of new dimensions,
Cheating checkmate by painting the king's robe
So that he slides like a queen;
Or to cry, 'Nightmare, nightmare!'
Like a corpse in the cholera-pit
Under a load of corpses;
Or to run the head against these blind walls,
Enter the dungeon, torment the eyes
With apparitions chained two and two,
And go frantic with fear—
To die and wake up sweating by moonlight
In the same courtyard, sleepless as before.

RETURN

The seven years' curse is ended now
That drove me forth from this kind land,
From mulberry-bough and apple-bough
And gummy twigs the west wind shakes,
To drink the brine from crusted lakes
And grit my teeth on sand.

Now for your cold, malicious brain
And most uncharitable, cold heart,
You, too, shall clank the seven years' chain
On sterile ground for all time cursed
With famine's itch and flames of thirst,
The blank sky's counterpart.

The load that from my shoulder slips
Straightway upon your own is tied:
You, too, shall scorch your finger-tips
With scrabbling on the desert's face
Such thoughts I had of this green place,
Sent scapegoat for your pride.

Here, Robin on a tussock sits,
And Cuckoo with his call of hope
Cuckoos awhile, then off he flits,
While peals of dingle-dongle keep
Troop-discipline among the sheep
That graze across the slope.

A brook from fields of gentle sun,
Through the glade its water heaves,
The falling cone would well-nigh stun
That Squirrel wantonly lets drop
When up he scampers to tree-top
And dives among the green.

But no, I ask a surer peace
Than vengeance on you could provide.
So fear no ill from my release:
Be off, elude the curse, disgrace
Some other green and happy place—
This world of fools is wide.

THE BARDS

The bards falter in shame, their running verse
Stumbles, with marrow-bones the drunken diners
Pelt them for their delay.
It is a something fearful in the song
Plagues them—an unknown grief that like a churl
Goes commonplace in cowskin
And bursts unheralded, crowing and coughing,
An unpilled holly-club twirled in his hand,
Into their many-shielded, samite-curtained,
Jewel-bright hall where twelve kings sit at chess
Over the white-bronze pieces and the gold;
And by a gross enchantment
Flails down the rafters and leads off the queens—
The wild-swan-breasted, the rose-ruddy-cheeked
Raven-haired daughters of their admiration—
To stir his black pots and to bed on straw.

A LOST WORLD

'Dear love, why should you weep
    For time's remorseless way?
Though today die in sleep
    And be called yesterday,
    We love, we stay.'

'I weep for days that died
    With former love that shone
On a world true and wide
    Before this newer one
    Which yours shines on.'

'Is this world not as true
    As that one ever was
Which now has fled from you
    Like shadows from the grass
    When the clouds pass?'

'Yet for that would I weep
    Kindly, before we kiss:
Love has a faith to keep
    With past felicities
    That weep for this.'

NOBODY

Nobody, ancient mischief, nobody,
Harasses always with an absent body.

Nobody coming up the road, nobody,
Like a tall man in a dark cloak, nobody.

Nobody about the house, nobody,
Like children creeping up the stairs, nobody.

Nobody anywhere in the garden, nobody,
Like a young girl quiet with needlework, nobody.

Nobody coming, nobody, not yet here,
Incessantly welcomed by the wakeful ear.

Until this nobody shall consent to die
Under his curse must everybody lie—

The curse of his envy, of his grief and fright,
Of sudden rape and murder screamed in the night.

THE PROGRESS

There is a travelling fury in his feet
  (Scorn for the waters of his native spring)
   Which proves at last the downfall of this king:
Shame will not let him sound the long retreat.

Tormented by his progress he displays
  An open flank to the swarmed enemy
   Who, charging through and through, set his pride free
For death's impossible and footless ways.

FULL MOON

As I walked out that sultry night,
  I heard the stroke of One.
The moon, attained to her full height,
  Stood beaming like the sun:
She exorcized the ghostly wheat
To mute assent in love's defeat,
  Whose tryst had now begun.

The fields lay sick beneath my tread,
  A tedious owlet cried,
A nightingale above my head
  With this or that replied—
Like man and wife who nightly keep
Inconsequent debate in sleep
  As they dream side by side.

Your phantom wore the moon's cold mask,
  My phantom wore the same;
Forgetful of the feverish task
  In hope of which they came,
Each image held the other's eyes
And watched a grey distraction rise
  To cloud the eager flame—

To cloud the eager flame of love,
  To fog the shining gate;
They held the tyrannous queen above
  Sole mover of their fate,
They glared as marble statues glare
Across the tessellated stair
  Or down the halls of state.

And now warm earth was Arctic sea,
  Each breath came dagger-keen;
Two bergs of glinting ice were we,
  The broad moon sailed between;
There swam the mermaids, tailed and finned,
And love went by upon the wind
  As though it had not been.

VANITY

Be assured, the Dragon is not dead
But once more from the pools of peace
Shall rear his fabulous green head.

The flowers of innocence shall cease
And like a harp the wind shall roar
And the clouds shake an angry fleece.

'Here, here is certitude,' you swore,
'Below this lightning-blasted tree.
Where once it struck, it strikes no more.

'Two lovers in one house agree.
The roof is tight, the walls unshaken.
As now, so must it always be.'

Such prophecies of joy awaken
The toad who dreams away the past
Under your hearth-stone, light forsaken,

Who knows that certitude at last
Must melt away in vanity—
No gate is fast, no door is fast—

That thunder bursts from the blue sky,
That gardens of the mind fall waste,
That fountains of the heart run dry.

PURE DEATH

We looked, we loved, and therewith instantly
Death became terrible to you and me.
By love we disenthralled our natural terror
From every comfortable philosopher
Or tall, grey doctor of divinity:
Death stood at last in his true rank and order.

It happened soon, so wild of heart were we,
Exchange of gifts grew to a malady:
Their worth rose always higher on each side
Till there seemed nothing but ungivable pride
That yet remained ungiven, and this degree
Called a conclusion not to be denied.

Then we at last bethought ourselves, made shift
And simultaneously this final gift
Gave: each with shaking hands unlocks
The sinister, long, brass-bound coffin-box,
Unwraps pure death, with such bewilderment
As greeted our love's first acknowledgement.

SICK LOVE

O Love, be fed with apples while you may,
And feel the sun and go in royal array,
A smiling innocent on the heavenly causeway,

Though in what listening horror for the cry
That soars in outer blackness dismally,
The dumb blind beast, the paranoiac fury:

Be warm, enjoy the season, lift your head,
Exquisite in the pulse of tainted blood,
That shivering glory not to be despised.

Take your delight in momentariness,
Walk between dark and dark—a shining space
With the grave's narrowness, though not its peace.

IT WAS ALL VERY TIDY

When I reached his place,
The grass was smooth,
The wind was delicate,
The wit well timed,
The limbs well formed,
The pictures straight on the wall:
It was all very tidy.

He was cancelling out
The last row of figures,
He had his beard tied up in ribbons,
There was no dust on his shoe,
Everyone nodded:
It was all very tidy.

Music was not playing,
There were no sudden noises,
The sun shone blandly,
The clock ticked:
It was all very tidy.

'Apart from and above all this,'
I reassured myself,
'There is now myself.'

It was all very tidy.

Death did not address me,
He had nearly done:
It was all very tidy.
They asked, did I not think
It was all very tidy?

I could not bring myself
To laugh, or untie
His beard's neat ribbons,
Or jog his elbow,
Or whistle, or sing,
Or make disturbance.
I consented, frozenly,
He was unexceptionable:
It was all very tidy.

III

CALLOW CAPTAIN

The sun beams jovial from an ancient sky,
  Flooding the round hills with heroic spate.
A callow captain, glaring, sword at thigh,
  Trots out his charger through the camp gate.
Soon comes the hour, his marriage hour, and soon
  He fathers children, reigns with ancestors
Who, likewise serving in the wars, won
  For a much-tattered flag renewed honours.

A wind ruffles the book, and he whose name
  Was mine vanishes; all is at an end.
Fortunate soldier: to be spared shame
  Of chapter-years unprofitable to spend,
To ride off into reticence, nor throw
  Before the story-sun a long shadow.

THIEF

To the galleys, thief, and sweat your soul out
With strong tugging under the curled whips,
That there your thievishness may find full play.
Whereas, before, you stole rings, flowers and watches,
Oaths, jests and proverbs,
Yet paid for bed and board like an honest man,
This shall be entire thiefdom: you shall steal
Sleep from chain-galling, diet from sour crusts,
Comradeship from the damned, the ten-year-chained—
And, more than this, the excuse for life itself
From a craft steered toward battles not your own.

THE FURIOUS VOYAGE

So, overmasterful, to sea!
But hope no distant view of sail,
No growling ice, nor weed, nor whale,
Nor breakers perilous on the lee.

Though you enlarge your angry mind
Three leagues and more about the ship
And stamp till every puncheon skip,
The wake runs evenly behind.

And it has width enough for you,
This vessel, dead from truck to keel,
With its unmanageable wheel,
Its blank chart and the surly crew,

In ballast only due to fetch
The turning point of wretchedness
On an uncoasted, featureless
And barren ocean of blue stretch.

SONG: LIFT-BOY

Let me tell you the story of how I began:
I began as the boot-boy and ended as the boot-man,
With nothing in my pockets but a jack-knife and a button,
With nothing in my pockets but a jack-knife and a button,
With nothing in my pockets.

Let me tell you the story of how I went on:
I began as the lift-boy and ended as the lift-man,
With nothing in my pockets but a jack-knife and a button,
With nothing in my pockets but a jack-knife and a button,
With nothing in my pockets.

I found it very easy to whistle and play
With nothing in my head or my pockets all day,
With nothing in my pockets.

But along came Old Eagle, like Moses or David,
He stopped at the fourth floor and preached me Damnation:
'Not a soul shall be savèd, not one shall be savèd.
The whole First Creation shall forfeit salvation:
From knife-boy to lift-boy, from ragged to regal,
Not one shall be savèd, not you, not Old Eagle,
No soul on earth escapeth, even if all repent——'
So I cut the cords of the lift and down we went,
With nothing in our pockets.

TRAVELLER'S CURSE AFTER
MISDIRECTION
(*from the Welsh*)

May they stumble, stage by stage
On an endless pilgrimage,
Dawn and dusk, mile after mile,
At each and every step, a stile;
At each and every step withal
May they catch their feet and fall;
At each and every fall they take
May a bone within them break;
And may the bone that breaks within
Not be, for variation's sake,
Now rib, now thigh, now arm, now shin,
But always, without fail, THE NECK.

THE LAST DAY OF LEAVE
(1916)

We five looked out over the moor
At rough hills blurred with haze, and a still sea:
Our tragic day, bountiful from the first.

We would spend it by the lily lake
(High in a fold beyond the farthest ridge),
Following the cart-track till it faded out.

The time of berries and bell-heather;
Yet all that morning nobody went by
But shepherds and one old man carting turfs.

We were in love: he with her, she with him,
And I, the youngest one, the odd man out,
As deep in love with a yet nameless muse.

No cloud; larks and heath-butterflies,
And herons undisturbed fishing the streams;
A slow cool breeze that hardly stirred the grass.

When we hurried down the rocky slope,
A flock of ewes galloping off in terror,
There shone the waterlilies, yellow and white.

Deep water and a shelving bank.
Off went our clothes and in we went, all five,
Diving like trout between the lily groves.

The basket had been nobly filled:
Wine and fresh rolls, chicken and pineapple—
Our braggadocio under threat of war.

The fire on which we boiled our kettle
We fed with ling and rotten blackthorn root;
And the coffee tasted memorably of peat.

Two of us might stray off together
But never less than three kept by the fire,
Focus of our uncertain destinies.

We spoke little, our minds in tune—
A sigh or laugh would settle any theme;
The sun so hot it made the rocks quiver.

But when it rolled down level with us,
Four pairs of eyes sought mine as if appealing
For a blind-fate-aversive afterword:—

'Do you remember the lily lake?
We were all there, all five of us in love,
Not one yet killed, widowed or broken-hearted.'

THE NEXT TIME

And that inevitable accident
   On the familiar journey—roughly reckoned
By miles and shillings—in a cramped compartment
   Between a first hereafter and a second?

And when we passengers are given two hours,
   The wheels failing once more at Somewhere-Nowhere,
To climb out, stretch our legs and pick wild flowers—
   Suppose that this time I elect to stay there?

ULYSSES

To the much-tossed Ulysses, never done
  With woman whether gowned as wife or whore,
Penelope and Circe seemed as one:
She like a whore made his lewd fancies run,
  And wifely she a hero to him bore.

Their counter-changings terrified his way:
  They were the clashing rocks, Symplegades,
Scylla and Charybdis too were they;
Now they were storms frosting the sea with spray
  And now the lotus island's drunken ease.

They multiplied into the Sirens' throng,
  Forewarned by fear of whom he stood bound fast
Hand and foot helpless to the vessel's mast,
Yet would not stop his ears: daring their song
  He groaned and sweated till that shore was past.

One, two and many: flesh had made him blind,
  Flesh had one pleasure only in the act,
Flesh set one purpose only in the mind—
Triumph of flesh and afterwards to find
  Still those same terrors wherewith flesh was racked.

His wiles were witty and his fame far known,
Every king's daughter sought him for her own,
  Yet he was nothing to be won or lost.
  All lands to him were Ithaca: love-tossed
He loathed the fraud, yet would not bed alone.

THE SUCCUBUS

Thus will despair
In ecstasy of nightmare
Fetch you a devil-woman through the air,
  To slide below the sweated sheet
And kiss your lips in answer to your prayer
  And lock her hands with yours and your feet with her feet.

Yet why does she
Come never as longed-for beauty
Slender and cool, with limbs lovely to see,
  (The bedside candle guttering high)
And toss her head so the thick curls fall free
  Of halo'd breast, firm belly and long, slender thigh?

Why with hot face,
With paunched and uddered carcase,
Sudden and greedily does she embrace,
  Gulping away your soul, she lies so close,
Fathering you with brats of her own race?
  Yet is the fancy grosser than your lusts were gross?

THE READER OVER MY SHOULDER

You, reading over my shoulder, peering beneath
My writing arm—I suddenly feel your breath
   Hot on my hand or on my nape,
So interrupt my theme, scratching these few
Words on the margin for you, namely you,
   Too-human shape fixed in that shape:—

All the saying of things against myself
And for myself I have well done myself.
   What now, old enemy, shall you do
But quote and underline, thrusting yourself
Against me, as ambassador of myself,
   In damned confusion of myself and you?

For you in strutting, you in sycophancy,
Have played too long this other self of me,
   Doubling the part of judge and patron
With that of creaking grind-stone to my wit.
Know me, have done: I am a proud spirit
   And you for ever clay. Have done.

THE LEGS

There was this road,
And it led up-hill,
And it led down-hill,
And round and in and out.

And the traffic was legs,
Legs from the knees down,
Coming and going,
Never pausing.

And the gutters gurgled
With the rain's overflow,
And the sticks on the pavement
Blindly tapped and tapped.

What drew the legs along
Was the never-stopping,
And the senseless, frightening
Fate of being legs.

Legs for the road,
The road for legs,
Resolutely nowhere
In both directions.

My legs at least
Were not in that rout:
On grass by the roadside
Entire I stood,

Watching the unstoppable
Legs go by
With never a stumble
Between step and step.

Though my smile was broad
The legs could not see,
Though my laugh was loud
The legs could not hear.

My head dizzied, then:
I wondered suddenly,
Might I too be a walker
From the knees down?

Gently I touched my shins.
The doubt unchained them:
They had run in twenty puddles
Before I regained them.

GARDENER

Loveliest flowers, though crooked in their border,
And glorious fruit, dangling from ill-pruned boughs—
Be sure the gardener had not eye enough
To wheel a barrow between the broadest gates
Without a clumsy scraping.

Yet none could think it simple awkwardness;
And when he stammered of a garden-guardian,
Said the smooth lawns came by angelic favour,
The pinks and pears in spite of his own blunders,
They nudged at this conceit.

Well, he had something, though he called it nothing—
An ass's wit, a hairy-belly shrewdness
That would appraise the intentions of the angel
By the very yard-stick of his own confusion,
And bring the most to pass.

FRONT DOOR SOLILOQUY

'Yet from the antique heights or deeps of what
Or which was grandeur fallen, sprung or what
Or which, beyond doubt I am grandeur's grandson
True to the eagle nose, the pillared neck,
(Missed by the intervening generation)
Whom large hands, long face, and long feet sort out
From which and what, to wear my heels down even,
To be connected with all reigning houses,
Show sixteen quarterings or sixty-four
Or even more, with clear skin and eyes clear
To drive the nails in and not wound the wood,
With lungs and heart sound and with bowels easy,
An angry man, heaving the sacks of grain
From cart to loft and what and what and which
And even thus, and being no Rousseauist,
Nor artists-of-the-world-unite, or which,
Or what, never admitting, in effect,
Touch anything my touch does not adorn—
Now then I dung on my grandfather's doorstep,
Which is a reasonable and loving due
To hold no taint of spite or vassalage
And understood only by him and me—
But you, you bog-rat-whiskered, you psalm-griddling,
Lame, rotten-livered, which and what canaille,
You, when twin lackeys, with armorial shovels,
Unbolt the bossy gates and bend to the task,
Be off, work out your heads from between the railings,
Lest we unkennel the mastiff and the Dane—
This house is jealous of its nastiness.'

IN BROKEN IMAGES

He is quick, thinking in clear images;
I am slow, thinking in broken images.

He becomes dull, trusting to his clear images;
I become sharp, mistrusting my broken images.

Trusting his images, he assumes their relevance;
Mistrusting my images, I question their relevance.

Assuming their relevance, he assumes the fact;
Questioning their relevance, I question the fact.

When the fact fails him, he questions his senses;
When the fact fails me, I approve my senses.

He continues quick and dull in his clear images;
I continue slow and sharp in my broken images.

He in a new confusion of his understanding;
I in a new understanding of my confusion.

TRUDGE, BODY!

Trudge, body, and climb, trudge and climb,
But not to stand again on any peak of time:
Trudge, body!

I'll cool you, body, with a hot sun, that draws the sweat,
I'll warm you, body, with ice-water, that stings the blood,
I'll enrage you, body, with idleness, to do
And having done to sleep the long night through:
Trudge, body!

But in such cooling, warming, doing or sleeping,
No pause for satisfaction: henceforth you make address
Beyond heat to the heat, beyond cold to the cold,
Beyond enraged idleness to enraged idleness.
With no more hours of hope, and none of regret,
Before each sun may rise, you salute it for set:
Trudge, body!

THE CHRISTMAS ROBIN

The snows of February had buried Christmas
Deep in the woods, where grew self-seeded
The fir-trees of a Christmas yet unknown,
Without a candle or a strand of tinsel.

Nevertheless when, hand in hand, plodding
Between the frozen ruts, we lovers paused
And 'Christmas trees!' cried suddenly together,
Christmas was there again, as in December.

We velveted our love with fantasy
Down a long vista-row of Christmas trees,
Whose coloured candles slowly guttered down
As grandchildren came trooping round our knees.

But he knew better, did the Christmas robin—
The murderous robin with his breast aglow
And legs apart, in a spade-handle perched:
He prophesied more snow, and worse than snow.

ON RISING EARLY

Rising early and walking in the garden
Before the sun has properly climbed the hill—
His rays warming the roof, not yet the grass
That is white with dew still.

And not enough breeze to eddy a puff of smoke,
And out in the meadows a thick mist lying yet,
And nothing anywhere ill or noticeable—
Thanks indeed for that.

But was there ever a day with wit enough
To be always early, to draw the smoke up straight
Even at three o'clock of an afternoon,
To spare dullness or sweat?

Indeed, many such days I remember
That were dew-white and gracious to the last,
That ruled out meal-times, yet had no more hunger
Than was felt by rising a half-hour before breakfast,
Nor more fatigue—where was it that I went
So unencumbered, with my feet trampling
Like strangers on the past?

FLYING CROOKED

The butterfly, a cabbage-white,
(His honest idiocy of flight)
Will never now, it is too late,
Master the art of flying straight,
Yet has—who knows so well as I?—
A just sense of how not to fly:
He lurches here and here by guess
And God and hope and hopelessness.
Even the aerobatic swift
Has not his flying-crooked gift.

FRAGMENT OF A LOST POEM

O the clear moment, when from the mouth
A word flies, current immediately
Among friends; or when a loving gift astounds
As the identical wish nearest the heart;
Or when a stone, volleyed in sudden danger,
Strikes the rabid beast full on the snout!

Moments in never . . .

BROTHER

It's odd enough to be alive with others,
But odder still to have sisters and brothers:
To make one of a characteristic litter—
The sisters puzzled and vexed, the brothers vexed and bitter
That this one wears, though flattened by abuse,
The family nose for individual use.

IV

GALATEA AND PYGMALION

Galatea, whom his furious chisel
From Parian stone had by greed enchanted,
Fulfilled, so they say, Pygmalion's longings:
    Stepped from the pedestal on which she stood,
Bare in his bed laid her down, lubricious,
With low responses to his drunken raptures,
    Enroyalled his body with her demon blood,

Alas, Pygmalion had so well plotted
The articulation of his woman monster
That schools of eager connoisseurs beset
    Her single person with perennial suit;
Whom she (a judgement on the jealous artist)
Admitted rankly to a comprehension
    Of themes that crowned her own, not his repute.

THE DEVIL'S ADVICE TO
STORY-TELLERS

Lest men suspect your tale to be untrue,
Keep probability—some say—in view.
But my advice to story-tellers is:
Weigh out no gross of probabilities,
Nor yet make diligent transcriptions of
Known instances of virtue, crime or love.
To forge a picture that will pass for true,
Do conscientiously what liars do—
Born liars, not the lesser sort that raid
The mouths of others for their stock-in-trade:
Assemble, first, all casual bits and scraps
That may shake down into a world perhaps;
People this world, by chance created so,
With random persons whom you do not know—
The teashop sort, or travellers in a train
Seen once, guessed idly at, not seen again;
Let the erratic course they steer surprise
Their own and your own and your readers' eyes;
Sigh then, or frown, but leave (as in despair)
Motive and end and moral in the air;
Nice contradiction between fact and fact
Will make the whole read human and exact.

SERGEANT-MAJOR MONEY
(1917)

It wasn't our battalion, but we lay alongside it,
  So the story is as true as the telling is frank.
They hadn't one Line-officer left, after Arras,
  Except a batty major and the Colonel, who drank.

'B' Company Commander was fresh from the Depôt,
  An expert on gas drill, otherwise a dud;
So Sergeant-Major Money carried on, as instructed,
  And that's where the swaddies began to sweat blood.

His Old Army humour was so well-spiced and hearty
  That one poor sod shot himself, and one lost his wits;
But discipline's maintained, and back in rest-billets
  The Colonel congratulates 'B' company on their kits.

The subalterns went easy, as was only natural
  With a terror like Money driving the machine,
Till finally two Welshmen, butties from the Rhondda,
  Bayoneted their bugbear in a field-canteen.

Well, we couldn't blame the officers, they relied on Money;
  We couldn't blame the pitboys, their courage was grand;
Or, least of all, blame Money, an old stiff surviving
  In a New (bloody) Army he couldn't understand.

SEA SIDE

Into a gentle wildness and confusion,
Of here and there, of one and everyone,
Of windy sandhills by an unkempt sea,
Came two and two in search of symmetry,
Found symmetry of two in sea and sand,
In left foot, right foot, left hand and right hand.

The beast with two backs is a single beast,
Yet by his love of singleness increased
To two and two and two and two again,
Until, instead of sandhills, see, a plain
Patterned in two and two, by two and two—
And the sea parts in horror at a view
Of rows of houses coupling, back to back,
While love smokes from their common chimney-stack
With two-four-eight-sixteenish single same
Re-registration of the duple name.

WM. BRAZIER

At the end of Tarriers' Lane, which was the street
We children thought the pleasantest in Town
Because of the old elms growing from the pavement
And the crookedness, when the other streets were straight,
[They were always at the lamp-post round the corner,
Those pugs and papillons and in-betweens,
Nosing and snuffling for the latest news]
Lived Wm. Brazier, with a gilded sign,
'Practical Chimney Sweep'. He had black hands,
Black face, black clothes, black brushes and white teeth;
He jingled round the town in a pony-trap,
And the pony's name was Soot, and Soot was black.
But the brass fittings on the trap, the shafts,
On Soot's black harness, on the black whip-butt,
Twinkled and shone like any guardsman's buttons.
Wasn't that pretty? And when we children jeered:
'Hello, Wm. Brazier! Dirty-face Wm. Brazier!'
He would crack his whip at us and smile and bellow,
'Hello, my dears!' [If he were drunk, but otherwise:
'Scum off, you damned young milliners' bastards, you!']

Let them copy it out on a pink page of their albums,
Carefully leaving out the bracketed lines.
It's an old story—f's for s's—
But good enough for them, the suckers.

WELSH INCIDENT

'But that was nothing to what things came out
From the sea-caves of Criccieth yonder.'
'What were they? Mermaids? dragons? ghosts?'
'Nothing at all of any things like that.'
'What were they, then?'
                    'All sorts of queer things,
Things never seen or heard or written about,
Very strange, un-Welsh, utterly peculiar
Things. Oh, solid enough they seemed to touch,
Had anyone dared it. Marvellous creation,
All various shapes and sizes, and no sizes,
All new, each perfectly unlike his neighbour,
Though all came moving slowly out together.'
'Describe just one of them.'
                        'I am unable.'
'What were their colours?'
                  'Mostly nameless colours,
Colours you'd like to see; but one was puce
Or perhaps more like crimson, but not purplish.
Some had no colour.'
                'Tell me, had they legs?'
'Not a leg nor foot among them that I saw.'
'But did these things come out in any order?
What o'clock was it? What was the day of the week?
Who else was present? How was the weather?'
'I was coming to that. It was half-past three
On Easter Tuesday last. The sun was shining.
The Harlech Silver Band played *Marchog Jesu*
On thirty-seven shimmering instruments,
Collecting for Caernarvon's (Fever) Hospital Fund.
The populations of Pwllheli, Criccieth,
Portmadoc, Borth, Tremadoc, Penrhyndeudraeth,
Were all assembled. Criccieth's mayor addressed them
First in good Welsh and then in fluent English,
Twisting his fingers in his chain of office,
Welcoming the things. They came out on the sand,
Not keeping time to the band, moving seaward
Silently at a snail's pace. But at last

The most odd, indescribable thing of all,
Which hardly one man there could see for wonder,
Did something recognizably a something.'
'Well, what?'
                        'It made a noise.'
                                        'A frightening noise?'
'No, no.'
                'A musical noise? A noise of scuffling?'
'No, but a very loud, respectable noise—
Like groaning to oneself on Sunday morning
In Chapel, close before the second psalm.'
'What did the mayor do?'
                                'I was coming to that'.

VISION IN THE REPAIR-SHOP

Be sure the crash was worse than ever.
In, flying out, collapsed with music;
Out, flying in, roared up in flames.
The blast was non-continuous.
But what matter? The force generated
At every point of impact
Was, you remarked, dispersed for other uses.
In this you saw the well-geared mind
Of the garage-man-in-chief,
Prime corpse of each new speed-track,
Who by unequalled salesmanship
Engines a car for every son and daughter
In a city of twelve millions—
What prettier traffic-block imaginable
Lasting, day in, day out, for centuries,
While life flows easily down the gutters
Or swings in the air on ropes,
And you and I, stuffing this cotton-wool
Closer into our ears, from habit,
Lie in plaster of Paris on our backs
And drink the drip of many radiators?

INTERRUPTION

If ever against this easy blue and silver
Hazed-over countryside of thoughtfulness,
Far behind in the mind and above,
Boots from before and below approach tramping,
Watch how their premonition will display
A forward countryside, low in the distance—
A picture-postcard square of June grass;
Will warm a summer season, trim the hedges,
Cast the river about on either flank,
Start the late cuckoo emptily calling,
Invent a rambling tale of moles and voles,
Furnish a path with stiles.
Watch how the field will broaden, the feet nearing,
Sprout with great dandelions and buttercups,
Widen and heighten. The blue and silver
Fogs at the border of this all-grass.
Interruption looms gigantified,
Lurches against, treads thundering through,
Blots the landscape, scatters all,
Roars and rumbles like a dark tunnel,
Is gone.
          The picture-postcard grass and trees
Swim back to central: it is a large patch,
It is a modest, failing patch of green,
The postage-stamp of its departure,
Clouded with blue and silver, closing in now
To a plain countryside of less and less,
Unpeopled and unfeatured blue and silver,
Before, behind, above.

You call the old nurse and the little page
To act survivors on your tragic stage—
You love the intrusive extra character.
'But where's the tragedy,' you say, 'if none
Remains to moralize on what's been done?
There's no catharsis in complete disaster.
Tears purge the soul—the nurse's broken line:
"O mistress, pretty one, dead!" the page's whine:
"Thou too? Alas, fond master!" '

No purge for my disgusted soul, no tears
Will wash away my bile of tragic years,
No sighs vicariously abate my rancour—
If nurse and page survive, I'd have them own
Small sorrow to be left up-stage alone,
And on the bloodiest field of massacre
Either rant out the anti-climax thus:
' 'A's dead, the bitch!' 'So's Oscar! Joy for us!'
Then fall to rifling pocket, belt and purse
With corky jokes and pantomime of sin;
Or let the feud rage on, page against nurse—
His jewelled dirk, her thund'rous rolling-pin.

MIDWAY

Between insufferable monstrosities
And exiguities insufferable,
Midway is man's own station. We no longer
Need either hang our heads or lift them high
But for the fortunes of finance or love.
We have no truck either with the forebeings
Of Betelgeux or with the atom's git.
Our world steadies: untrembling we renew
Old fears of earthquakes, adders, floods, mad dogs
And all such wholesomes. Nothing that we do
Concerns the infinities of either scale.
Clocks tick with our consent to our time-tables,
Trains run between our buffers. Time and Space
Amuse us merely with their rough-house turn,
Their hard head-on collision in the tunnel.
A dying superstition smiles and hums
'Abide with me'—God's evening prayer, not ours.
So history still is written and is read:
The eternities of divine commonplace.

HELL

Husks, rags and bones, waste-paper, excrement,
   Denied a soul whether for good or evil
And casually consigned to unfulfilment,
   Are pronged into his bag by the great-devil.

Or words repeated, over and over and over,
   Until their sense sickens and all but dies,
These the same fellow like a ghoulish lover
   Will lay his hands upon and hypnotize.

From husks and rags and waste and excrement
   He forms the pavement-feet and the lift-faces;
He steers the sick words into parliament
   To rule a dust-bin world with deep-sleep phrases.

When healthy words or people chance to dine
   Together in this rarely actual scene,
There is a love-taste in the bread and wine,
   Nor is it asked: 'Do you mean what you mean?'

But to their table-converse boldly comes
   The same great-devil with his brush and tray,
To conjure plump loaves from the scattered crumbs,
   And feed his false five thousands day by day.

LEDA

Heart, with what lonely fears you ached,
   How lecherously mused upon
That horror with which Leda quaked
   Under the spread wings of the swan.

Then soon your mad religious smile
   Made taut the belly, arched the breast,
And there beneath your god awhile
   You strained and gulped your beastliest.

Pregnant you are, as Leda was,
   Of bawdry, murder and deceit;
Perpetuating night because
   The after-languors hang so sweet.

SYNTHETIC SUCH

'The sum of all the parts of Such—
    Of each laboratory scene—
Is Such.' While Science means this much
    And means no more, why, let it mean!

But were the science-men to find
    Some animating principle
Which gave synthetic Such a mind
    Vital, though metaphysical—

To Such, such an event, I think
    Would cause unscientific pain:
Science, appalled by thought, would shrink
    To its component parts again.

THE FLORIST ROSE

This wax-mannequin nude, the florist rose,
She of the long stem and too glossy leaf,
Is dead to honest greenfly and leaf-cutter:
Behind plate-glass watches the yellow fogs.

Claims kin with the robust male aeroplane
Whom eagles hate and phantoms of the air,
Who has no legend, as she breaks from legend—
From fellowship with sword and sail and crown.

Experiment's flower, scentless (he its bird);
Is dewed by the spray-gun; is tender-thorned;
Pouts, false-virginal, between bud and bloom;
Bought as a love-gift, droops within the day.

LOST ACRES

These acres, always again lost
  By every new ordnance-survey
And searched for at exhausting cost
  Of time and thought, are still away.

They have their paper-substitute—
  Intercalation of an inch
At the so-many-thousandth foot:
  And no one parish feels the pinch.

But lost they are, despite all care,
  And perhaps likely to be bound
Together in a piece somewhere,
  A plot of undiscovered ground.

Invisible, they have the spite
  To swerve the tautest measuring-chain
And the exact theodolite
  Perched every side of them in vain.

Yet, be assured, we have no need
  To plot these acres of the mind
With prehistoric fern and reed
  And monsters such as heroes find.

Maybe they have their flowers, their birds,
  Their trees behind the phantom fence,
But of a substance without words:
  To walk there would be loss of sense.

AT FIRST SIGHT

'Love at first sight,' some say, misnaming
Discovery of twinned helplessness
Against the huge tug of procreation.

But friendship at first sight? This also
Catches fiercely at the surprised heart
So that the cheek blanches and then blushes.

RECALLING WAR

Entrance and exit wounds are silvered clean,
The track aches only when the rain reminds.
The one-legged man forgets his leg of wood,
The one-armed man his jointed wooden arm.
The blinded man sees with his ears and hands
As much or more than once with both his eyes.
Their war was fought these twenty years ago
And now assumes the nature-look of time,
As when the morning traveller turns and views
His wild night-stumbling carved into a hill.

What, then, was war? No mere discord of flags
But an infection of the common sky
That sagged ominously upon the earth
Even when the season was the airiest May.
Down pressed the sky, and we, oppressed, thrust out
Boastful tongue, clenched fist and valiant yard.
Natural infirmities were out of mode,
For Death was young again: patron alone
Of healthy dying, premature fate-spasm.

Fear made fine bed-fellows. Sick with delight
At life's discovered transitoriness,
Our youth became all-flesh and waived the mind.
Never was such antiqueness of romance,
Such tasty honey oozing from the heart.
And old importances came swimming back—
Wine, meat, log-fires, a roof over the head,
A weapon at the thigh, surgeons at call.
Even there was a use again for God—
A word of rage in lack of meat, wine, fire,
In ache of wounds beyond all surgeoning.

War was return of earth to ugly earth,
War was foundering of sublimities,
Extinction of each happy art and faith
By which the world had still kept head in air,
Protesting logic or protesting love,
Until the unendurable moment struck—
The inward scream, the duty to run mad.

And we recall the merry ways of guns—
Nibbling the walls of factory and church
Like a child, piecrust; felling groves of trees
Like a child, dandelions with a switch.
Machine-guns rattle toy-like from a hill,
Down in a row the brave tin-soldiers fall:
A sight to be recalled in elder days
When learnedly the future we devote
To yet more boastful visions of despair.

DOWN, WANTON, DOWN!

Down, wanton, down! Have you no shame
That at the whisper of Love's name,
Or Beauty's, presto! up you raise
Your angry head and stand at gaze?

Poor bombard-captain, sworn to reach
The ravelin and effect a breach—
Indifferent what you storm or why,
So be that in the breach you die!

Love may be blind, but Love at least
Knows what is man and what mere beast;
Or Beauty wayward, but requires
More delicacy from her squires.

Tell me, my witless, whose one boast
Could be your staunchness at the post,
When were you made a man of parts
To think fine and profess the arts?

Will many-gifted Beauty come
Bowing to your bald rule of thumb,
Or Love swear loyalty to your crown?
Be gone, have done! Down, wanton, down!

A FORMER ATTACHMENT

And glad to find, on again looking at it,
It meant even less to me than I had thought—
You know the ship is moving when you see
The boxes on the quayside sliding away
And growing smaller—and feel a calm delight
When the port's cleared and the coast out of sight,
And ships are few, each on its proper course,
With no occasion for approach or discourse.

NATURE'S LINEAMENTS

When mountain rocks and leafy trees
And clouds and things like these,
With edges,

Caricature the human face,
Such scribblings have no grace
Nor peace—

The bulbous nose, the sunken chin,
The ragged mouth in grin
Of cretin.

Nature is always so: you find
That all she has of mind
Is wind,

Retching among the empty spaces,
Ruffling the idiot grasses,
The sheep's fleeces.

Whose pleasures are excreting, poking,
Havocking and sucking,
Sleepy licking.

Whose griefs are melancholy,
Whose flowers are oafish,
Whose waters, silly,
Whose birds, raffish,
Whose fish, fish.

TIME

The vague sea thuds against the marble cliffs
And from their fragments age-long grinds
Pebbles like flowers.

Or the vague weather wanders in the fields,
And up spring flowers with coloured buds
Like marble pebbles.

The beauty of the flowers is Time, death-grieved;
The pebbles' beauty too is Time,
Life-wearied.

It is easy to admire a blowing flower
Or a smooth pebble flower-like freaked
By Time and vagueness.

Time is Time's lapse, the emulsive element coaxing
All obstinate locks and rusty hinges
To loving-kindness.

And am I proof against that lovesome pair,
Old age and childhood, twins in Time,
In sorrowful vagueness?

And will I not pretend the accustomed thanks:
Humouring age with filial flowers,
Childhood with pebbles?

THE PHILOSOPHER

Three blank walls, a barred window with no view,
A ceiling within reach of the raised hands,
A floor blank as the walls.

And, ruling out distractions of the body—
Growth of the hair and nails, a prison diet,
Thoughts of escape—

Ruling out memory and fantasy,
The distant tramping of a gaoler's boots,
Visiting mice and such,

What solace here for a laborious mind!
What a redoubtable and single task
One might attempt here:

Threading a logic between wall and wall,
Ceiling and floor, more accurate by far
Than the cob-spider's.

Truth captured without increment of flies—
Spinning and knotting till the cell became
A spacious other head

In which the emancipated reason might
Learn in due time to walk at greater length
And more unanswerably.

ON DWELLING

Courtesies of good-morning and good-evening
From rustic lips fail as the town encroaches:
Soon nothing passes but the cold quick stare
Of eyes that see ghosts, yet too many for fear.

Here I too walk, silent myself, in wonder
At a town not mine though plainly coextensive
With mine, even in days coincident:
In mine I dwell, in theirs like them I haunt.

And the green country, should I turn again there?
My bumpkin neighbours loom even ghostlier:
Like trees they murmur or like blackbirds sing
Courtesies of good-morning and good-evening.

HOTEL BED AT LUGANO

Even in hotel beds the hair tousles.
But this is observation, not complaint—
'Complaints should please be dropped in the complaint-box'—
'Which courteously we beg you to vacate
In that clean state as you should wish to find it.'

And the day after Carnival, today,
I found, in the square, a crimson cardboard heart:
'Anna Maria', it read. Otherwise, friends,
No foreign news—unless that here they drink
Red wine from china bowls; here anis-roots
Are stewed like turnips; here funiculars
Light up at dusk, two crooked constellations;
And if bells peal a victory or great birth,
That will be cows careering towards the pail.

'It is not yet the season,' pleads the Porter,
'That comes in April, when the rain most rains.'
Trilingual Switzer fish in Switzer lakes
Pining for rain and bread-crumbs of the season,
In thin reed-beds you pine!

                          A-bed drowsing,
(While the hair slowly tousles) uncomplaining . . .
Anna Maria's heart under my pillow
Provokes no furious dream. Who is this Anna?
A Switzer maiden among Switzer maidens,
Child of the children of that fox who never
Ate the sour grapes: her teeth not set on edge.

OGRES AND PYGMIES

Those famous men of old, the Ogres—
They had long beards and stinking arm-pits,
They were wide-mouthed, long-yarded and great-bellied
Yet not of taller stature, Sirs, than you.
They lived on Ogre-Strand, which was no place
But the churl's terror of their vast extent,
Where every foot was three-and-thirty inches
And every penny bought a whole hog.
Now of their company none survive, not one,
The times being, thank God, unfavourable
To all but nightmare shadows of their fame;
Their images stand howling on the hill
(The winds enforced against those wide mouths),
Whose granite haunches country-folk salute
With May Day kisses, and whose knobbed knees.

So many feats they did to admiration:
With their enormous throats they sang louder
Than ten cathedral choirs, with their grand yards
Stormed the most rare and obstinate maidenheads,
With their strong-gutted and capacious bellies
Digested stones and glass like ostriches.
They dug great pits and heaped huge mounds,
Deflected rivers, wrestled with the bear
And hammered judgements for posterity—
For the sweet-cupid-lipped and tassel-yarded
Delicate-stomached dwellers
In Pygmy Alley, where with brooding on them
A foot is shrunk to seven inches
And twelve-pence will not buy a spare rib.
And who would judge between Ogres and Pygmies—
The thundering text, the snivelling commentary—
Reading between such covers he will marvel
How his own members bloat and shrink again.

HISTORY OF THE WORD

The Word that in the beginning was the Word
For two or three, but elsewhere spoke unheard,
Found Words to interpret it, which for a season
Prevailed until ruled out by Law and Reason
Which, by a lax interpretation cursed,
In Laws and Reasons logically dispersed;
These, in their turn, found they could do no better
Than fall to Letters and each claim a letter.
In the beginning then, the Word alone,
But now the various tongue-tied Lexicon
In perfect impotence the day nearing
When every ear shall lose its sense of hearing
And every mind by knowledge be close-shuttered—
But two or three, that hear the Word uttered.

SINGLE FARE

By way of Fishguard, all the lying devils
Are back to Holy Ireland whence they came.
Each took a single fare: which cost them less
And brought us comfort. The dumb devils too
Take single fares, return by rail to Scotland
Whence they came. So the air is cool and easy.
And if, in some quarter of some big city,
A little Eire or a little Scotland
Serves as a rallying-point for a few laggards,
No matter, we are free from taint of them.
And at the fire-side now (drinking our coffee),
If I ask, 'But to what township did they book,
Those dumb devils of Scotland?' you will answer:
'There's the Bass Rock, once more a separate kingdom,
Leagued with Ireland, the same cold grey crag
Screamed against by the gulls that are all devils.'
And of the Irish devils you will answer:
'In Holy Ireland many a country seat
Still stands unburned—as Cooper's Hill, Lisheen,
Cloghan Castle, or Killua in County Galway—
For the devils to enter, unlock the library doors
And write love-letters and long threatening letters
Even to us, if it so pleases them.'

TO WALK ON HILLS

To walk on hills is to employ legs
As porters of the head and heart
Jointly adventuring towards
Perhaps true equanimity.

To walk on hills is to see sights
And hear sounds unfamiliar.
When in wind the pine-tree roars,
When crags with bleatings echo,
When water foams below the fall,
Heart records that journey
As memorable indeed;
Head reserves opinion,
Confused by the wind.

A view of three shires and the sea!
Seldom so much at once appears
Of the coloured world, says heart.
Head is glum, says nothing.

Legs become weary, halting
To sprawl in a rock's shelter,
While the sun drowsily blinks
On head at last brought low—
This giddied passenger of legs
That has no word to utter.

Heart does double duty,
As heart, and as head,
With portentous trifling.
A castle, on its crag perched,
Across the miles between is viewed
With awe as across years.

Now a daisy pleases,
Pleases and astounds, even,
That on a garden lawn could blow
All summer long with no esteem.

And the buzzard's cruel poise,
And the plover's misery,
And the important beetle's
Blue-green-shiny back . . .

To walk on hills is to employ legs
To march away and lose the day.
Confess, have you known shepherds?
And are they not a witless race,
Prone to quaint visions?
Not thus from solitude
(Solitude sobers only)
But from long hilltop striding.

TO BRING THE DEAD TO LIFE

To bring the dead to life
Is no great magic.
Few are wholly dead:
Blow on a dead man's embers
And a live flame will start.

Let his forgotten griefs be now,
And now his withered hopes;
Subdue your pen to his handwriting
Until it prove as natural
To sign his name as yours.

Limp as he limped,
Swear by the oaths he swore;
If he wore black, affect the same;
If he had gouty fingers,
Be yours gouty too.

Assemble tokens intimate of him—
A seal, a cloak, a pen:
Around these elements then build
A home familiar to
The greedy revenant.

So grant him life, but reckon
That the grave which housed him
May not be empty now:
You in his spotted garments
Shall yourself lie wrapped.

TO EVOKE POSTERITY

To evoke posterity
Is to weep on your own grave,
Ventriloquizing for the unborn:
'Would you were present in flesh, hero!
What wreaths and junketings!'

And the punishment is fixed:
To be found fully ancestral,
To be cast in bronze for a city square,
To dribble green in times of rain
And stain the pedestal.

Spiders in the spread beard;
A life proverbial
On clergy lips a-cackle;
Eponymous institutes,
Their luckless architecture.

Two more dates of life and birth
For the hour of special study
From which all boys and girls of mettle
Twice a week play truant
And worn excuses try.

Alive, you have abhorred
The crowds on holiday
Jostling and whistling—yet would you air
Your death-mask, smoothly lidded,
Along the promenade?

ANY HONEST HOUSEWIFE

Any honest housewife could sort them out,
Having a nose for fish, an eye for apples.
Is it any mystery who are the sound,
And who the rotten? Never, by her lights.

Any honest housewife who, by ill-fortune,
Ever engaged a slut to scrub for her
Could instantly distinguish from the workers
The lazy, the liars, and the petty thieves.

Does this denote a sixth peculiar sense
Gifted to housewives for their vestal needs?
Or is it failure of the usual five
In all unthrifty writers on this head?

DEFEAT OF THE REBELS

The enemy forces are in wild flight.
Poor souls (you say), they were intoxicated
With rhetoric and banners, thought it enough
To believe and to blow trumpets, to wear
That menacing lie in their shakos.

Enough: it falls on us to shoot them down,
The incorrigibles and cowards,
Where they shiver behind rocks, or in ditches
Seek graves that have no headstones to them—
Such prisoners were unprofitable.

Now as our vanguard, pressing on,
Dislodges them from village and town,
Who yelling abandon packs and cloaks,
Their arms and even the day's rations,
We are not abashed by victory,

We raise no pitying monument
To check the counter-stroke of fortune.
These are not spoils: we recognize
Our own strewn gear, that never had been robbed
But for our sloth and hesitancy.

NEVER SUCH LOVE

Twined together and, as is customary,
For words of rapture groping, they
'Never such love,' swore, 'ever before was!'
Contrast with all loves that had failed or staled
Registered their own as love indeed.

And was this not to blab idly
The heart's fated inconstancy?
Better in love to seal the love-sure lips,
For truly love was before words were,
And no word given, no word broken.

When the name 'love' is uttered
(Love, the near-honourable malady
With which in greed and haste they
Each other do infect and curse)
Or, worse, is written down . . .

Wise after the event, by love withered,
A 'never more!' most frantically
Sorrow and shame would proclaim
Such as, they'd swear, never before were:
True lovers even in this.

THE FALLEN SIGNPOST

The signpost of four arms is down,
But one names your departure-town:
With this for guide you may replant
Your post and choose which road you want—

Logic that only seems obscure
To those deliberately not sure
Whether a journey should begin
With cross-roads or with origin.

The square post, and the socket square—
Now which way round to set it there?
Thus from the problem coaxing out
Four further elements of doubt,

They make the simple cross-roads be
A crux of pure dubiety
Demanding how much more concern
Than to have taken the wrong turn!

THE CHINA PLATE

From a crowded barrow in a street-market
The plate was ransomed for a few coppers,
Was brought gleefully home, given a place
On a commanding shelf.

'Quite a museum-piece,' an expert cries
(Eyeing it through the ready pocket-lens)—
As though a glass case would be less sepulchral
Than the barrow-hearse!

For weeks this plate retells the history
Whenever an eye runs in that direction:
'Near perdition I was, in a street-market
With rags and old shoes.'

'A few coppers'—here once again
The purchaser's proud hand lifts down
The bargain, displays the pot-bank sign
Scrawled raggedly underneath.

Enough, permit the treasure to forget
The emotion of that providential purchase,
Becoming a good citizen of the house
Like its fellow-crockery.

Let it dispense sandwiches at a party
And not be noticed in the drunken buzz,
Or little cakes at afternoon tea
When cakes are in demand.

Let it regain a lost habit of life,
Foreseeing death in honourable breakage
Somewhere between the kitchen and the shelf—
To be sincerely mourned.

CERTAIN MERCIES

Now must all satisfaction
Appear mere mitigation
Of an accepted curse?

Must we henceforth be grateful
That the guards, though spiteful,
Are slow of foot and wit?

That by night we may spread
Over the plank bed
A thin coverlet?

That the rusty water
In the unclean pitcher
Our thirst quenches?

That the rotten, detestable
Food is yet eatable
By us ravenous?

That the prison censor
Permits a weekly letter?
(We may write: 'we are well.')

That, with patience and deference,
We do not experience
The punishment cell?

That each new indignity
Defeats only the body,
Pampering the spirit
With obscure, proud merit?

THE CUIRASSIERS OF THE FRONTIER

Goths, Vandals, Huns, Isaurian mountaineers,
Made Roman by our Roman sacrament,
We can know little (as we care little)
Of the Metropolis: her candled churches,
Her white-gowned pederastic senators,
The cut-throat factions of her Hippodrome,
The eunuchs of her draped saloons.

Here is the frontier, here our camp and place—
Beans for the pot, fodder for horses,
And Roman arms. Enough. He who among us
At full gallop, the bowstring to his ear,
Lets drive his heavy arrows, to sink
Stinging through Persian corslets damascened,
Then follows with the lance—he has our love.

The Christ bade Holy Peter sheathe his sword,
Being outnumbered by the Temple guard.
And this was prudence, the cause not yet lost
While Peter might persuade the crowd to rescue.
Peter renegued, breaking his sacrament.
With us the penalty is death by stoning,
Not to be made a bishop.

In Peter's Church there is no faith nor truth,
Nor justice anywhere in palace or court.
That we continue watchful on the rampart
Concerns no priest. A gaping silken dragon,
Puffed by the wind, suffices us for God.
We, not the City, are the Empire's soul:
A rotten tree lives only in its rind.

THE LAUREATE

Like a lizard in the sun, though not scuttling
When men approach, this wretch, this thing of rage,
Scowls and sits rhyming in his horny age.

His time and truth he has not bridged to ours,
But shrivelled by long heliotropic idling
He croaks at us his out-of-date humours.

Once long ago here was a poet; who died.
See how remorse twitching his mouth proclaims
It was no natural death, but suicide.

Arrogant, lean, unvenerable, he
Still turns for comfort to the western flames
That glitter a cold span above the sea.

A JEALOUS MAN

To be homeless is a pride
To the jealous man prowling
Hungry down the night lanes,

Who has no steel at his side,
No drink hot in his mouth,
But a mind dream-enlarged,

Who witnesses warfare,
Man with woman, hugely
Raging from hedge to hedge:

The raw knotted oak-club
Clenched in the raw fist,
The ivy-noose well flung,

The thronged din of battle,
Gaspings of the throat-snared,
Snores of the battered dying,

Tall corpses, braced together,
Fallen in clammy furrows,
Male and female,

Or, among haulms of nettle
Humped, in noisome heaps,
Male and female.

He glowers in the choked roadway
Between twin churchyards,
Like a turnip ghost.

(Here, the rain-worn headstone,
There, the Celtic cross
In rank white marble.)

This jealous man is smitten,
His fear-jerked forehead
Sweats a fine musk;

A score of bats bewitched
By the ruttish odour
Swoop singing at his head;

Nuns bricked up alive
Within the neighbouring wall
Wail in cat-like longing.

Crow, cocks, crow loud,
Reprieve the doomed devil——
Has he not died enough?

Now, out of careless sleep,
She wakes and greets him coldly,
The woman at home,

She, with a private wonder
At shoes bemired and bloody—
His war was not hers.

THE CLOAK

Into exile with only a few shirts,
Some gold coin and the necessary papers.
But winds are contrary: the Channel packet
Time after time returns the sea-sick peer
To Sandwich, Deal or Rye. He does not land,
But keeps his cabin; so at last we find him
In humble lodgings maybe at Dieppe,
His shirts unpacked, his night-cap on a peg,
Passing the day at cards and swordsmanship
Or merry passages with chambermaids,
By night at his old work. And all is well—
The country wine wholesome although so sharp,
And French his second tongue; a faithful valet
Brushes his hat and brings him newspapers.
This nobleman is at home anywhere,
His castle being, the valet says, his title.
The cares of an estate would incommode
Such tasks as now his Lordship has in hand.
His Lordship, says the valet, contemplates
A profitable absence of some years.
Has he no friend at Court to intercede?
He wants none: exile's but another name
For an old habit of non-residence
In all but the recesses of his cloak.
It was this angered a great personage.

THE FOREBODING

Looking by chance in at the open window
  I saw my own self seated in his chair
With gaze abstracted, furrowed forehead,
  Unkempt hair.

I thought that I had suddenly come to die,
  That to a cold corpse this was my farewell,
Until the pen moved slowly upon paper
  And tears fell.

He had written a name, yours, in printed letters:
  One word on which bemusedly to pore—
No protest, no desire, your naked name,
  Nothing more.

Would it be to-morrow, would it be next year?
  But the vision was not false, this much I knew;
And I turned angrily from the open window
  Aghast at you.

Why never a warning, either by speech or look,
  That the love you cruelly gave me could not last?
Already it was too late: the bait swallowed,
  The hook fast.

WITH HER LIPS ONLY

This honest wife, challenged at dusk
At the garden gate, under a moon perhaps,
In scent of honeysuckle, dared to deny
Love to an urgent lover: with her lips only,
Not with her heart. It was no assignation;
Taken aback, what could she say else?
For the children's sake, the lie was venial;
'For the children's sake', she argued with her conscience.

Yet a mortal lie must follow before dawn:
Challenged as usual in her own bed,
She protests love to an urgent husband,
Not with her heart but with her lips only;
'For the children's sake', she argues with her conscience,
'For the children'—turning suddenly cold towards them.

THE HALLS OF BEDLAM

Forewarned of madness:
In three days' time at dusk
The fit masters him.

How to endure those days?
(Forewarned is foremad)
'—Normally, normally.'

He will gossip with children,
Argue with elders,
Check the cash account.

'I shall go mad that day—'
The gossip, the argument,
The neat marginal entry.

His case is not uncommon,
The doctors pronounce;
But prescribe no cure.

To be mad is not easy,
Will earn him no more
Than a niche in the news.

Then to-morrow, children,
To-morrow or the next day
He resigns from the firm.

His boyhood's ambition
Was to become an artist—
Like any City man's.

To the walls and halls of Bedlam
The artist is welcome—
Bold brush and full palette.

Through the cell's grating
He will watch his children
To and from school.

'Suffer the little children
To come unto me
With their Florentine hair!'

A very special story
For their very special friends—
They burst in the telling:

Of an evil thing, armed,
Tap-tapping on the door,
Tap-tapping on the floor,
'On the third day at dusk.'

Father in his shirt-sleeves
Flourishing a hatchet—
Run, children, run!

No one could stop him,
No one understood;
And in the evening papers . . .

(Imminent genius,
Troubles at the office,
Normally, normally,
As if already mad.)

OR TO PERISH BEFORE DAY

The pupils of the eye expand
And from near-nothings build up sight;
The pupil of the heart, the ghost,
Swelling parades the dewy land:

With cowardice and with self-esteem
Makes terror in the track that through
The fragrant spotted pasture runs;
And a bird wails across the dream.

Now, if no heavenly window shines
Nor angel-voices cheer the way,
The ghost will overbear the man
And mark his head with fever-signs.

The flowers of dusk that he has pulled
To wonder at when morning's here
Are snail-shells upon straws of grass—
So easily the eye is gulled.

The sounding words that his mouth fill
Upon to-morrow's lip shall droop;
The legs that slide with skating ease
Be stiff to the awakened will.

Or, should he perish before day,
He leaves his lofty ghost behind
Perpetuating uncontrolled
This hour of glory and dismay.

A COUNTRY MANSION

This ancient house so notable
For its gables and great staircase,
Its mulberry-trees and alleys of clipped yew,
Humbles the show of every near demesne.

At the beginning it acknowledged owners—
Father, son, grandson—
But then, surviving the last heirs of the line,
Became a place for life-tenancy only.

At the beginning, no hint of fate,
No rats and no hauntings;
In the garden, then, the fruit-trees grew
Slender and similar in long rows.

A bedroom with a low ceiling
Caused little fret at first;
But gradual generations of discomfort
Have bred an anger there to stifle sleep.

And the venerable dining-room,
Where port in Limerick glasses
Glows twice as red reflected
In the memory-mirror of the waxed table—

For a time with paint and flowered paper
A mistress tamed its walls,
But pious antiquarian hands, groping,
Rediscovered the grey panels beneath.

Children love the old house tearfully,
And the parterres, how fertile!
Married couples under the testers hugging
Enjoy carnality's bliss as nowhere else.

A smell of mould from loft to cellar,
Yet sap still brisk in the oak
Of the great beams: if ever they use a saw
It will stain, as cutting a branch from a green tree.

. . . Old Parr had lived one hundred years and five
(So to King Charles he bragged)
When he did open penance, in a sheet,
For fornication with posterity.

Old Parr died; not so the mansion
Whose inhabitants, bewitched,
Pour their fresh blood through its historic veins
And, if a tile blow from the roof, tremble.

The last-born of this race of sacristans
Broke the long spell, departed;
They lay his knife and fork at every meal
And every evening warm his bed;

Yet cannot draw him back from the far roads
For trifling by the lily-pool
Or wine at the hushed table where they meet,
The guests of genealogy.

It was his childhood's pleasure-ground
And still may claim his corpse,
Yet foster-cradle or foster-grave
He will not count as home.

This rebel does not hate the house,
Nor its dusty joys impugn:
No place less reverend could provoke
So proud an absence from it.

He has that new malaise of time:
Gratitude choking with vexation
That he should opulently inherit
The goods and titles of the extinct.

LOVERS IN WINTER

The posture of the tree
  Shows the prevailing wind;
And ours, long misery
  When you are long unkind.

But forward, look, we lean—
  Not backward as in doubt—
And still with branches green
  Ride our ill weather out.

ADVOCATES

Fugitive firs and larches for a moment
Caught, past midnight, by our headlight beam
On that mad journey through unlasting lands
I cannot put a name to, years ago,
(And my companions drowsy-drunk)—these trees
Resume again their sharp appearance, perfect
Of spur and tassel, claiming memory,
Claiming affection: 'Will we be included
In the catalogue? Yes, yes?' they plead.

Green things, you are already there enrolled.
And should a new resentment gnaw in me
Against my dear companions of that journey
(Strangers already then, in thought and deed)
You shall be advocates, charged to deny
That all the good I lived with them is lost.

V

ON PORTENTS

If strange things happen where she is,
So that men say that graves open
And the dead walk, or that futurity
Becomes a womb and the unborn are shed,
Such portents are not to be wondered at,
Being tourbillions in Time made
By the strong pulling of her bladed mind
Through that ever-reluctant element.

THE TERRACED VALLEY

In a deep thought of you and concentration
I came by hazard to a new region:
The unnecessary sun was not there,
The necessary earth lay without care—
For more than sunshine warmed the skin
Of the round world that was turned outside-in.

Calm sea beyond the terraced valley
Without horizon easily was spread,
As it were overhead,
Washing the mountain-spurs behind me:
The unnecessary sky was not there,
Therefore no heights, no deeps, no birds of the air.

Neat outside-inside, neat below-above,
Hermaphrodizing love.
Neat this-way-that-way and without mistake:
On the right hand could slide the left glove.
Neat over-under: the young snake
Through an unyielding shell his path could break.
Singing of kettles, like a singing brook,
Made out-of-doors a fireside nook.

But you, my love, where had you then your station?
Seeing that on this counter-earth together
We go not distant from each other;
I knew you near me in that strange region,
So searched for you, in hope to see you stand
On some near olive-terrace, in the heat,
The left-hand glove drawn on your right hand,
The empty snake's egg perfect at your feet—

But found you nowhere in the wide land,
And cried disconsolately, until you spoke
Immediate at my elbow, and your voice broke
This trick of time, changing the world about
To once more inside-in and outside-out.

ALEXANDER AND QUEEN JANET

On Janet come so late
To their banquet of state
   The angels nobly smile;
But Alexander thrusts away his plate.

'Janet, where have you been?
Janet, what have you seen?
   Your lover is abashed:
For want of you we have sat down thirteen.'

'I have nowhere been,
And nothing have I seen.
   Were it not for Alexander
You had no reason to sit down thirteen.'

Sweet wine for Janet now,
Fresh costards from the bough
   Of Paradise, white bread
Which they must force between her lips somehow.

'I could not wish,' says she,
'For prettier company,
   Angels of light, than yours,
Yet crystal cups and dishes are not for me.

'Though Alexander dine
On Heaven's own bread and wine,
   And Paradisal fruit,
Such delicacies are not for me or mine.

'Do you approve the grace
Of my form or my face?
   It springs from earth,' says Janet,
'And must be welcomed in a greener place.'

At this the angels hide
Their proud heads, mortified;
　　Being deep in love with Janet
And jealous, too, for Alexander's pride.

Queen Janet softly goes
Treading on her tip toes
　　To the bright table head;
She lays before her man a damask rose.

'Is it still your desire
To shiver at my fire?
　　Then come now, Alexander,
Or stay and be a monk, or else a friar.'

'My lambkin, my sweet,
I have dined on angels' meat,
　　And in you I had trusted
To attend their call and make my joy complete.'

'Do you come? Do you stay?
Alexander, say!
　　For if you will not come
This gift rose I must surely snatch away.'

'Janet, how can I come?
Eat only a crumb
　　Of bread, essay this wine!
In God's name sit beside me; or be dumb.'

Her back Janet turns,
Dumbly she spurns
　　The red rose with her shoe;
But in each cheek another red rose burns.

The twelve angels, alas,
Are brought to a sad pass:
    Their lucent plumage pales,
Their glittering sapphire eyes go dull as glass.

Now Alexander's soul
Flies up from the brain hole,
    To circle like a bat
Above his body threshing past control.

It was Queen Janet's power
Turned the sweet wine sour,
    Shrivelled the apples' bloom,
And the bread crumbled into dusty flour.

THE CHINK

A sunbeam on the well-waxed oak,
  In shape resembling not at all
The ragged chink by which it broke
  Into this darkened hall,
Swims round and golden over me,
The sun's plenipotentiary.

So may my round love a chink find:
  With such address to break
Into your grief-occluded mind
  As you shall not mistake
  But, rising, open to me for truth's sake.

THE AGES OF OATH

To find a garden-tulip growing
Among wild primroses of a wild field,
Or a cuckoo's egg in a blackbird's nest,
Or a giant mushroom, a whole basketful—
The memorable feats of childhood!
Once, by the earthworks, scratching in the soil,
My stick turned up a Roman amber bead . . .

The lost, the freakish, the unspelt
Drew me: for simple sights I had no eye.
And did I swear allegiance then
To wildness, not (as I thought) to truth—
Become a virtuoso, and this also,
Later, of simple sights, when tiring
Of unicorn and upas?

Did I forget how to greet plainly
The especial sight, how to know deeply
The pleasure shared by upright hearts?
And is this to begin afresh, with oaths
On the true book, in the true name,
Now stammering out my praise of you,
Like a boy owning his first love?

NEW LEGENDS

Content in you,
Andromeda serene,
Mistress of air and ocean
And every fiery dragon,
Chained to no cliff,
Asking no rescue of me.

Content in you,
Mad Atalanta,
Stooping unpausing,
Ever ahead,
Acquitting me of rivalry.

Content in you
Who made King Proteus marvel,
Showing him singleness
Past all variety.

Content in you,
Niobe of no children,
Of no calamity.

Content in you,
Helen, foiler of beauty.

LIKE SNOW

She, then, like snow in a dark night,
Fell secretly. And the world waked
With dazzling of the drowsy eye,
So that some muttered 'Too much light,'
And drew the curtains close.
Like snow, warmer than fingers feared,
And to soil friendly;
Holding the histories of the night
In yet unmelted tracks.

END OF PLAY

We have reached the end of pastime, for always,
Ourselves and everyone, though few confess it
Or see the sky other than, as of old,
A foolish smiling Mary-mantle blue;

Though life may still seem to dawdle golden
In some June landscape among giant flowers,
The grass to shine as cruelly green as ever,
Faith to descend in a chariot from the sky—

May seem only: a mirror and an echo
Mediate henceforth with vision and sound.
The cry of faith, no longer mettlesome,
Sounds as a blind man's pitiful plea of 'blind'.

We have at last ceased idling, which to regret
Were as shallow as to ask our milk-teeth back;
As many forthwith do, and on their knees
Call lugubriously upon chaste Christ.

We tell no lies now, at last cannot be
The rogues we were—so evilly linked in sense
With what we scrutinized that lion or tiger
Could leap from every copse, strike and devour us.

No more shall love in hypocritic pomp
Conduct its innocents through a dance of shame,
From timid touching of gloved fingers
To frantic laceration of naked breasts.

Yet love survives, the word carved on a sill
Under antique dread of the headsman's axe;
It is the echoing mind, as in the mirror
We stare on our dazed trunks at the block kneeling.

THE CLIMATE OF THOUGHT

The climate of thought has seldom been described.
It is no terror of Caucasian frost,
Nor yet that brooding Hindu heat
For which a loin-rag and a dish of rice
Suffice until the pestilent monsoon.
But, without winter, blood would run too thin;
Or, without summer, fires would burn too long.
In thought the seasons run concurrently.

Thought has a sea to gaze, not voyage, on;
And hills, to rough the edge of the bland sky,
Not to be climbed in search of blander prospect;
Few birds, sufficient for such caterpillars
As are not fated to turn butterflies;
Few butterflies, sufficient for such flowers
As are the luxury of a full orchard;
Wind, sometimes, in the evening chimneys; rain
On the early morning roof, on sleepy sight;
Snow streaked upon the hilltop, feeding
The fond brook at the valley-head
That greens the valley and that parts the lips;
The sun, simple, like a country neighbour;
The moon, grand, not fanciful with clouds.

THE FALLEN TOWER OF SILOAM

Should the building totter, run for an archway!
We were there already—already the collapse
Powdered the air with chalk, and shrieking
Of old men crushed under the fallen beams
Dwindled to comic yelps. How unterrible
When the event outran the alarm
And suddenly we were free—

Free to forget how grim it stood,
That tower, and what wide fissures ran
Up the west wall, how rotten the under-pinning
At the south-eastern angle. Satire
Had whirled a gentle wind around it,
As if to buttress the worn masonry;
Yet we, waiting, had abstained from satire.

It behoved us, indeed, as poets
To be silent in Siloam, to foretell
No visible calamity. Though kings
Were crowned and gold coin minted still and horses
Still munched at nose-bags in the public streets,
All such sad emblems were to be condoned:
An old wives' tale, not ours.

THE GREAT-GRANDMOTHER

That aged woman with the bass voice
And yellowing white hair: believe her.
Though to your grandfather, her son, she lied
And to your father disingenuously
Told half the tale as the whole,
Yet she was honest with herself,
Knew disclosure was not yet due,
Knows it is due now.

She will conceal nothing of consequence
From you, her great-grandchildren
(So distant the relationship,
So near her term),
Will tell you frankly, she has waited
Only for your sincere indifference
To exorcize that filial regard
Which has estranged her, seventy years,
From the folk of her house.

Confessions of old distaste
For music, sighs and roses—
Their false-innocence assaulting her,
Breaching her hard heart;
Of the pleasures of a full purse,
Of clean brass and clean linen,
Of being alone at last;
Disgust with the ailing poor
To whom she was bountiful;
How the prattle of young children
Vexed more than if they whined;
How she preferred cats.

She will say, yes, she acted well,
Took such pride in the art
That none of them suspected, even,
Her wrathful irony
In doing what they asked
Better than they could ask it . . .
But, ah, how grudgingly her will returned
After the severance of each navel-cord,
And fled how far again,
When again she was kind!

She has outlasted all man-uses,
As was her first resolve:
Happy and idle like a port
After the sea's recession,
She does not misconceive the nature
Of shipmen or of ships.
Hear her, therefore, as the latest voice;
The intervening generations (drifting
On tides of fancy still), ignore.

NO MORE GHOSTS

The patriarchal bed with four posts
Which was a harbourage of ghosts
Is hauled out from the attic glooms
And cut to wholesome furniture for wholesome rooms;

Where they (the ghosts) confused, abused, thinned,
Forgetful how they sighed and sinned,
Cannot disturb our ordered ease
Except as summer dust tickles the nose to sneeze.

We are restored to simple days, are free
From cramps of dark necessity,
And one another recognize
By an immediate love that signals at our eyes.

No new ghosts can appear. Their poor cause
Was that time freezes, and time thaws;
But here only such loves can last
As do not ride upon the weathers of the past.

VI

A LOVE STORY

The full moon easterly rising, furious,
Against a winter sky ragged with red;
The hedges high in snow, and owls raving—
Solemnities not easy to withstand:
A shiver wakes the spine.

In boyhood, having encountered the scene,
I suffered horror: I fetched the moon home,
With owls and snow, to nurse in my head
Throughout the trials of a new Spring,
Famine unassuaged.

But fell in love, and made a lodgement
Of love on those chill ramparts.
Her image was my ensign: snows melted,
Hedges sprouted, the moon tenderly shone,
The owls trilled with tongues of nightingale.

These were all lies, though they matched the time,
And brought me less than luck: her image
Warped in the weather, turned beldamish.
Then back came winter on me at a bound,
The pallid sky heaved with a moon-quake.

Dangerous it had been with love-notes
To serenade Queen Famine.
In tears I recomposed the former scene,
Let the snow lie, watched the moon rise, suffered the owls,
Paid homage to them of unevent.

DAWN BOMBARDMENT

Guns from the sea open against us:
The smoke rocks bodily in the casemate
And a yell of doom goes up.
We count and bless each new, heavy concussion—
Captives awaiting rescue.

Visiting angel of the wild-fire hair
Who in dream reassured us nightly
Where we lay fettered,
Laugh at us, as we wake—our faces
So tense with hope the tears run down.

THE WORMS OF HISTORY

On the eighth day God died; his bearded mouth
That had been shut so long flew open.
So Adam's too in a dismay like death—
But the world still rolled on around him,
Instinct with all those lesser powers of life
That God had groaned against but not annulled.

'All-Excellent', Adam had titled God,
And in his mourning now demeaned himself
As if all excellence, not God, had died;
Chose to be governed by those lesser powers,
More than inferior to excellence—
The worms astir in God's corrupt flesh.

God died, not excellence his name:
Excellence lived, but only was not God.
As for those lesser powers who played at God,
Bloated with Adam's deferential sighs
In mourning for expired divinity,
They reigned as royal monsters upon earth.

Adam grew lean, and wore perpetual black;
He made no reaching after excellence.
Eve gave him sorry comfort for his grief
With birth of sons, and mourning still he died.
Adam was buried in one grave with God
And the worms ranged and ravaged in between.

Into their white maws fell abundance
Of all things rotten. They were greedy-nosed
To smell the taint out and go scavenging,
Yet over excellence held no domain.
Excellence lives; they are already dead—
The ages of a putrefying corpse.

THE GLUTTON

Beyond the Atlas roams a glutton
Lusty and sleek, a shameless robber,
Sacred to Aethiopian Aphrodite;
The aborigines harry it with darts,
And its flesh is esteemed, though of a fishy tang
Tainting the eater's mouth and lips.

Ourselves once, wandering in mid-wilderness
And by despair drawn to this diet,
Before the meal was over sat apart
Loathing each other's carrion company.

THE SHOT

The curious heart plays with its fears:
To hurl a shot through the ship's planks,
Being assured that the green angry flood
Is charmed and dares not dance into the hold—
Nor first to sweep a lingering glance around
For land or shoal or cask adrift.
'So miracles are done; but madmen drown.'

O weary luxury of hypothesis—
For human nature, honest human nature
(Which the fear-pampered heart denies)
Knows its own miracle: not to go mad.
Will pitch the shot in fancy, hint the fact,
Will bore perhaps a meagre auger hole
But stanch the spurting with a tarred rag,
And will not drown, nor even ride the cask.

THE THIEVES

Lovers in the act dispense
With such meum-tuum sense
As might warningly reveal
What they must not pick or steal,
And their nostrum is to say:
'I and you are both away.'

After, when they disentwine
You from me and yours from mine,
Neither can be certain who
Was that I whose mine was you.
To the act again they go
More completely not to know.

Theft is theft and raid is raid
Though reciprocally made.
Lovers, the conclusion is
Doubled sighs and jealousies
In a single heart that grieves
For lost honour among thieves.

LOLLOCKS

By sloth on sorrow fathered,
These dusty-featured Lollocks
Have their nativity in all disordered
Backs of cupboard drawers.

They play hide and seek
Among collars and novels
And empty medicine bottles,
And letters from abroad
That never will be answered.

Every sultry night
They plague little children,
Gurgling from the cistern,
Humming from the air,
Skewing up the bed-clothes,
Twitching the blind.

When the imbecile agèd
Are over-long in dying
And the nurse drowses,
Lollocks come skipping
Up the tattered stairs
And are nasty together
In the bed's shadow.

The signs of their presence
Are boils on the neck,
Dreams of vexation suddenly recalled
In the middle of the morning,
Languor after food.

Men cannot see them,
Men cannot hear them,
Do not believe in them—
But suffer the more
Both in neck and belly.

Women can see them—
O those naughty wives
Who sit by the fireside
Munching bread and honey,
Watching them in mischief
From corners of their eyes,
Slily allowing them to lick
Honey-sticky fingers.

Sovereign against Lollocks
Are hard broom and soft broom,
To well comb the hair,
To well brush the shoe,
And to pay every debt
As it falls due.

TO SLEEP

The mind's eye sees as the heart mirrors:
Loving in part, I did not see you whole,
Grew flesh-enraged that I could not conjure
A whole you to attend my fever-fit
In the doubtful hour between a night and day
And be Sleep that had kept so long away.

Of you sometimes a hand, a brooch, a shoe
Wavered beside me, unarticulated—
As the vexed insomniac dream-forges;
And the words I chose for your voice to speak
Echoed my own voice with its dry creak.

Now that I love you, now that I recall
All scattered elements of will that swooped
By night as jealous dreams through windows
To circle above the beds like bats,
Or as dawn-birds flew blindly at the panes
In curiosity rattling out their brains—

Now that I love you, as not before,
Now you can be and say, as not before:
The mind clears and the heart true-mirrors you
Where at my side an early watch you keep
And all self-bruising heads loll into sleep.

DESPITE AND STILL

Have you not read
The words in my head,
And I made part
Of your own heart?
We have been such as draw
The losing straw—
You of your gentleness,
I of my rashness,
Both of despair—
Yet still might share
This happy will:
To love despite and still.
Never let us deny
The thing's necessity,
But, O, refuse
To choose
Where chance may seem to give
Loves in alternative.

THE SUICIDE IN THE COPSE

The suicide, far from content,
Stared down at his own shattered skull:
Was this what he meant?

Had not his purpose been
To liberate himself from duns and dolts
By a change of scene?

From somewhere came a roll of laughter:
He had looked so on his wedding-day,
And the day after.

There was nowhere at all to go,
And no diversion now but to peruse
What literature the winds might blow

Into the copse where his body lay:
A year-old sheet of sporting news,
A crumpled schoolboy essay.

FRIGHTENED MEN

We were not ever of their feline race,
Never had hidden claws so sharp as theirs
In any half-remembered incarnation;
Have only the least knowledge of their minds
Through a grace on their part in thinking aloud;
And we remain mouse-quiet when they begin
Suddenly in their unpredictable way
To weave an allegory of their lives,
Making each point by walking round it—
Then off again, as interest is warmed.
What have they said? Or unsaid? What?
We understood the general drift only.

They are punctilious as implacable,
Most neighbourly to those who love them least.
A shout will scare them. When they spring, they seize.
The worst is when they hide from us and change
To something altogether other:
We meet them at the door, as who returns
After a one-hour-seeming century
To a house not his own.

THE OATH

The doubt and the passion
Falling away from them,
   In that instant both
Take timely courage
From the sky's clearness
   To confirm an oath.

Her loves are his loves,
His trust is her trust;
   Else all were grief
And they, lost ciphers
On a yellowing page,
   Death overleaf.

Rumour of old battle
Growls across the air;
   Then let it growl
With no more terror
Than the creaking stair
   Or the calling owl.

She knows, as he knows,
Of a faithful-always
   And an always-dear
By early emblems
Prognosticated,
   Fulfilled here.

LANGUAGE OF THE SEASONS

Living among orchards, we are ruled
By the four seasons necessarily:
This from unseasonable frosts we learn
Or from usurping suns and haggard flowers—
Legitimist our disapproval.

Weather we knew, not seasons, in the city
Where, seasonless, orange and orchid shone,
Knew it by heavy overcoat or light,
Framed love in later terminologies
Than here, where we report how weight of snow,
Or weight of fruit, tears branches from the tree.

MID-WINTER WAKING

Stirring suddenly from long hibernation,
I knew myself once more a poet
Guarded by timeless principalities
Against the worm of death, this hillside haunting;
And presently dared open both my eyes.

O gracious, lofty, shone against from under,
Back-of-the-mind-far clouds like towers;
And you, sudden warm airs that blow
Before the expected season of new blossom,
While sheep still gnaw at roots and lambless go—

Be witness that on waking, this mid-winter,
I found her hand in mine laid closely
Who shall watch out the Spring with me.
We stared in silence all around us
But found no winter anywhere to see.

THE ROCK AT THE CORNER

The quarrymen left ragged
A rock at the corner;
But over it move now
The comforting fingers
Of ivy and briar.

Nor will it need assurance
Of nature's compassion
When presently it weathers
To a noble landmark
Of such countenance

That travellers in winter
Will see it as a creature
On guard at the corner
Where deep snows ingratiate
The comforts of death.

THE BEACH

Louder than gulls the little children scream
Whom fathers haul into the jovial foam;
But others fearlessly rush in, breast high,
Laughing the salty water from their mouths—
Heroes of the nursery.

The horny boatman, who has seen whales
And flying fishes, who has sailed as far
As Demerara and the Ivory Coast,
Will warn them, when they crowd to hear his tales,
That every ocean smells alike of tar.

THE VILLAGERS AND DEATH

The Rector's pallid neighbour at The Firs,
Death, did not flurry the parishioners.
Yet from a weight of superstitious fears
Each tried to lengthen his own term of years.
He was congratulated who combined
Toughness of flesh and weakness of the mind
In consequential rosiness of face.
This dull and not ill-mannered populace
Pulled off their caps to Death, as they slouched by,
But rumoured him both atheist and spy.
All vowed to outlast him (though none ever did)
And hear the earth drum on his coffin-lid.
Their groans and whispers down the village street
Soon soured his nature, which was never sweet.

THE DOOR

When she came suddenly in
It seemed the door could never close again,
Nor even did she close it—she, she—
The room lay open to a visiting sea
Which no door could restrain.

Yet when at last she smiled, tilting her head
To take her leave of me,
Where she had smiled, instead
There was a dark door closing endlessly,
The waves receded.

UNDER THE POT

Sulkily the sticks burn, and though they crackle
    With scorn under the bubbling pot, or spout
Magnanimous jets of flame against the smoke,
    At each heel end a dirty sap breaks out.

Confess, creatures, how sulkily ourselves
    We hiss with doom, fuel of a sodden age—
Not rapt up roaring to the chimney stack
    On incandescent clouds of spirit or rage.

THROUGH NIGHTMARE

Never be disenchanted of
That place you sometimes dream yourself into,
Lying at large remove beyond all dream,
Or those you find there, though but seldom
In their company seated—

The untameable, the live, the gentle.
Have you not known them? Whom? They carry
Time looped so river-wise about their house
There's no way in by history's road
To name or number them.

In your sleepy eyes I read the journey
Of which disjointedly you tell; which stirs
My loving admiration, that you should travel
Through nightmare to a lost and moated land,
Who are timorous by nature.

TO LUCIA AT BIRTH

Though the moon beaming matronly and bland
   Greets you, among the crowd of the new-born,
With 'welcome to the world' yet understand
   That still her pale, lascivious unicorn
And bloody lion are loose on either hand:
   With din of bones and tantarará of horn
Their fanciful cortège parades the land—
   Pest on the high road, wild-fire in the corn.

Outrageous company to be born into,
   Lunatics of a royal age long dead.
Then reckon time by what you are or do,
   Not by the epochs of the war they spread.
   Hark how they roar; but never turn your head.
Nothing will change them, let them not change you.

DEATH BY DRUMS

If I cried out in anger against music,
    It was not that I cried
Against the wholesome bitter arsenic
    Necessary for suicide:
For suicide in the drums' racking riot
    Where horned moriscoes wailing to their bride
Scare every Lydian songster from the spot.

SHE TELLS HER LOVE WHILE HALF ASLEEP

She tells her love while half asleep,
  In the dark hours,
    With half-words whispered low:
As Earth stirs in her winter sleep
  And puts out grass and flowers
    Despite the snow,
    Despite the falling snow.

THESEUS AND ARIADNE

High on his figured couch beyond the waves
He dreams, in dream recalling her set walk
Down paths of oyster-shell bordered with flowers
Across the shadowy turf below the vines.
He sighs: 'Deep sunk in my erroneous past
She haunts the ruins and the ravaged lawns.'

Yet still unharmed it stands, the regal house
Crooked with age and overtopped by pines
When first he wearied of her constancy.
And with a surer foot she goes than when
Dread of his hate was thunder in the air,
When the pines agonized with flaws of wind
And flowers glared up at her with frantic eyes.
Of him, now all is done, she never dreams
But calls a living blessing down upon
What he supposes rubble and rank grass;
Playing the queen to nobler company.

PENTHESILEIA

Penthesileia, dead of profuse wounds,
Was despoiled of her arms by Prince Achilles
Who, for love of that fierce white naked corpse,
Necrophily on her committed
In the public view.

Some gasped, some groaned, some bawled their indignation,
Achilles nothing cared, distraught by grief,
But suddenly caught Thersites' obscene snigger
And with one vengeful buffet to the jaw
Dashed out his life.

This was a fury few might understand,
Yet Penthesileia, hailed by Prince Achilles
On the Elysian plain, pauses to thank him
For avenging her insulted womanhood
With sacrifice.

COLD WEATHER PROVERB

Fearless approach and puffed feather
In birds, famine bespeak;
In man, belly filled full.

THE DEATH ROOM

Look forward, truant, to your second childhood.
The crystal sphere discloses
Wall-paper roses mazily repeated
In pink and bronze, their bunches harbouring
Elusive faces, under an inconclusive
Circling, spidery, ceiling craquelure,
And, by the window-frame, the well-loathed, lame,
Damp-patch, cross-patch, sleepless L-for-Lemur
Who, puffed to giant size,
Waits jealously till children close their eyes.

TO JUAN AT THE WINTER SOLSTICE

There is one story and one story only
That will prove worth your telling,
Whether as learned bard or gifted child;
To it all lines or lesser gauds belong
That startle with their shining
Such common stories as they stray into.

Is it of trees you tell, their months and virtues,
Or strange beasts that beset you,
Of birds that croak at you the Triple will?
Or of the Zodiac and how slow it turns
Below the Boreal Crown,
Prison of all true kings that ever reigned?

Water to water, ark again to ark,
From woman back to woman:
So each new victim treads unfalteringly
The never altered circuit of his fate,
Bringing twelve peers as witness
Both to his starry rise and starry fall.

Or is it of the Virgin's silver beauty,
All fish below the thighs?
She in her left hand bears a leafy quince;
When with her right she crooks a finger, smiling,
How may the King hold back?
Royally then he barters life for love.

Or of the undying snake from chaos hatched,
Whose coils contain the ocean,
Into whose chops with naked sword he springs,
Then in black water, tangled by the reeds,
Battles three days and nights,
To be spewed up beside her scalloped shore?

Much snow is falling, winds roar hollowly,
The owl hoots from the elder,
Fear in your heart cries to the loving-cup:
Sorrow to sorrow as the sparks fly upward.
The log groans and confesses:
There is one story and one story only.

Dwell on her graciousness, dwell on her smiling,
Do not forget what flowers
The great boar trampled down in ivy time.
Her brow was creamy as the crested wave,
Her sea-blue eyes were wild
But nothing promised that is not performed.

TO BE CALLED A BEAR

Bears gash the forest trees
  To mark the bounds
  Of their own hunting grounds;
They follow the wild bees
  Point by point home
  For love of honeycomb;
They browse on blueberries.

Then should I stare
If I am called a bear,
And it is not the truth?
Unkempt and surly with a sweet tooth
I tilt my muzzle toward the starry hub
Where Queen Callisto guards her cub;

But envy those that here
  All winter breathing slow
  Sleep warm under the snow,
That yawn awake when the skies clear,
  And lank with longing grow
No more than one brief month a year.

VII

MY NAME AND I

The impartial Law enrolled a name
   For my especial use:
My rights in it would rest the same
Whether I puffed it into fame
   Or sank it in abuse.

Robert was what my parents guessed
   When first they peered at me,
And *Graves* an honourable bequest
With Georgian silver and the rest
   From my male ancestry.

They taught me: 'You are *Robert Graves*
   (Which you must learn to spell),
But see that *Robert Graves* behaves,
Whether with honest men or knaves,
   Exemplarily well.'

Then though my I was always I,
   Illegal and unknown,
With nothing to arrest it by—
As will be obvious when I die
   And *Robert Graves* lives on—

I cannot well repudiate
   This noun, this natal star,
This gentlemanly self, this mate
So kindly forced on me by fate,
   Time and the registrar;

And therefore hurry him ahead
   As an ambassador
To fetch me home my beer and bread
Or commandeer the best green bed,
   As he has done before.

Yet, understand, I am not he
    Either in mind or limb;
My name will take less thought for me,
In worlds of men I cannot see,
    Than ever I for him.

At Viscount Nelson's lavish funeral,
   While the mob milled and yelled about St Paul's,
A General chatted with an Admiral:

'One of your Colleagues, Sir, remarked today
   That Nelson's *exit*, though to be lamented,
Falls not inopportunely, in its way.'

'He was a thorn in our flesh,' came the reply—
   'The most bird-witted, unaccountable,
Odd little runt that ever I did spy.

'One arm, one peeper, vain as Pretty Poll,
   A meddler, too, in foreign politics
And gave his heart in pawn to a plain moll.

'He would dare lecture us Sea Lords, and then
   Would treat his ratings as though men of honour
And play at leap-frog with his midshipmen!

'We tried to box him down, but up he popped,
   And when he'd banged Napoleon at the Nile
Became too much the hero to be dropped.

'You've heard that Copenhagen "blind eye" story?
   We'd tied him to Nurse Parker's apron-strings—
By G—d, he snipped them through and snatched the glory!'

'Yet,' cried the General, 'six-and-twenty sail
   Captured or sunk by him off Tráfalgár—
That writes a handsome *finis* to the tale.'

'Handsome enough. The seas are England's now.
   That fellow's foibles need no longer plague us.
He died most creditably, I'll allow.'

'And, Sir, the secret of his victories?'
   'By his unServicelike, familiar ways, Sir,
He made the whole Fleet love him, damn his eyes!'

AT THE SAVOY CHAPEL

[From *World's Press News*, 22 February, 1945. 'Alexander Clifford, the war correspondent, is today marrying Flight Officer Jenny Nicholson, daughter of Robert Graves. They met in the front line.']

Up to the wedding, formal with heirloom lace,
Press-cameras, carnations out of season,
Well-mellowed priest and well-trained choristers,

The relatives come marching, such as meet
Only at weddings and at funerals,
The elder generation with the eldest.

Family features for years undecided
What look to wear against a loveless world
Fix, as the wind veers, in the same grimace.

Each eyes the others with a furtive pity:
'Heavens, how she has aged—and he,
Grey hair and sunken cheeks, what a changed man!'

They stare wistfully at the bride (released
From brass buttons and the absurd salute)
In long white gown, bouquet and woman's pride.

'How suitable!' they whisper, and the whisper
'How suitable!' rustles from pew to pew;
To which I nod suitably grave assent.

Now for you, loving ones, who kneel at the altar
And preside afterwards at table—
The trophy sword that shears the cake recalling

What god you entertained last year together,
His bull neck looped with guts,
Trampling corpse-carpet through the villages—

Here is my private blessing: so to remain
As today you are, with features
Resolute and unchangeably your own.

DREAM OF A CLIMBER

Watch how this climber raises his own ladder
From earth to heaven, and not in a night
Nor from the secret, stony pillow.
(World patents pending; tested in the shops.)

Here's quality timber, nosings of pure brass,
The perfect phallo-spiritual tilt,
A fuzzy puff of cloud on top—
Excellent lure for angels and archangels!

Come, climber, with your scientific hat
And beady gambler's eye, ascend!
He pauses, poses for his camera-man:
'Well-known Climber About to Ascend.'

But in the published print, we may be sure,
He will appear, not on the lowest rung
But nearly out of view, almost in the cloud,
Leaning aside for an angel to pass,
His muscular broad hands a-glint in the sun,
And crampons on his feet.

THE PERSIAN VERSION

Truth-loving Persians do not dwell upon
The trivial skirmish fought near Marathon.
As for the Greek theatrical tradition
Which represents that summer's expedition
Not as a mere reconnaissance in force
By three brigades of foot and one of horse
(Their left flank covered by some obsolete
Light craft detached from the main Persian fleet)
But as a grandiose, ill-starred attempt
To conquer Greece—they treat it with contempt;
And only incidentally refute
Major Greek claims, by stressing what repute
The Persian monarch and the Persian nation
Won by this salutary demonstration:
Despite a strong defence and adverse weather
All arms combined magnificently together.

THE WEATHER OF OLYMPUS

Zeus was once overheard to shout at Hera:
   'You hate it, do you? Well, I hate it worse—
East wind in May, sirocco all the Summer.
   Hell take this whole impossible Universe!'

A scholiast explains his warm rejoinder,
   Which sounds too man-like for Olympic use,
By noting that the snake-tailed Chthonian winds
   Were answerable to Fate alone, not Zeus.

APOLLO OF THE PHYSIOLOGISTS

Despite this learned cult's official
And seemingly sincere denial
That they either reject or postulate
God, or God's scientific surrogate,
Prints of a deity occur *passim*
Throughout their extant literature. They make him
A dumb, dead-pan Apollo with a profile
Drawn in Victorian-Hellenistic style—
The pallid, bald, partitioned head suggesting
Wholly abstract cerebral functioning;
Or nude and at full length, this deity
Displays digestive, venous, respiratory
And nervous systems painted in bold colour
On his immaculate exterior.
Sometimes, *in verso*, a bald, naked Muse,
His consort, flaunts her arteries and sinews,
While, upside-down, crouched in her chaste abdomen,
Adored by men and wondered at by women,
Hangs a Victorian-Hellenistic foetus—
Fruit of her academic god's afflatus.

THE OLDEST SOLDIER

The sun shines warm on seven old soldiers
    Paraded in a row,
Perched like starlings on the railings—
    Give them plug-tobacco!

They'll croon you the Oldest-Soldier Song:
    Of Harry who took a holiday
From the sweat of ever thinking for himself
    Or going his own bloody way.

It was arms-drill, guard and kit-inspection,
    Like dreams of a long train-journey,
And the barrack-bed that Harry dossed on
    Went rockabye, rockabye, rockabye.

Harry kept his rifle and brasses clean,
    But Jesus Christ, what a liar!
He won the Military Medal
    For his coolness under fire.

He was never the last on parade
    Nor the first to volunteer,
And when Harry rose to be storeman
    He seldom had to pay for his beer.

Twenty-one years, and out Harry came
    To be odd-job man, or janitor,
Or commissionaire at a picture-house,
    Or, some say, bully to a whore.

But his King and Country calling Harry,
    He reported again at the Depôt,
To perch on this railing like a starling,
    The oldest soldier of the row.

GROTESQUES

I

My Chinese uncle, gouty, deaf, half-blinded,
And more than a trifle absent-minded,
Astonished all St James's Square one day
By giving long and unexceptionably exact directions
To a little coolie girl, who'd lost her way.

II

The Lion-faced Boy at the Fair
And the Heir Apparent
Were equally slow at remembering people's faces.
But whenever they met, incognito, in the Brazilian
Pavilion, the Row and such-like places,
They exchanged, it is said, their sternest nods—
Like gods of dissimilar races.

III

Dr Newman with the crooked pince-nez
Had studied in Vienna and Chicago.
Chess was his only relaxation.
And Dr Newman remained unperturbed
By every nastier manifestation
Of pluto-democratic civilization:
All that was cranky, corny, ill-behaved,
Unnecessary, askew or orgiastic
Would creep unbidden to his side-door (hidden
Behind a poster in the Tube Station,
Nearly half-way up the moving stairs),
Push its way in, to squat there undisturbed
Among box-files and tubular steel-chairs.

He was once seen at the Philharmonic Hall
Noting the reactions of two patients,
With pronounced paranoiac tendencies,
To old Dutch music. He appeared to recall
A tin of lozenges in his breast-pocket,
Put his hand confidently in—

And drew out a black imp, or sooterkin,
Six inches long, with one ear upside-down,
Licking at a vanilla ice-cream cornet—
Then put it back again with a slight frown.

IV

A Royal Duke, with no campaigning medals
To dignify his Orders, he would speak
Nostalgically at times of Mozambique
Where once the ship he cruised in ran aground:
How he drank cocoa, from a sailor's mug,
Poured from the common jug,
While loyal toasts went round.

V

Sir John addressed the Snake-god in his temple,
Which was full of bats, not as a votary
But with the somewhat cynical courtesy,
Just short of condescension,
He might have paid the Governor-General
Of a small, hot, backward colony.
He was well versed in primitive religion,
But found this an embarrassing occasion:
The God was immense, noisy and affable,
Began to tickle him with a nervous chuckle,
Unfobbed a great gold clock for him to listen,
Hissed like a snake, and swallowed him at one mouthful.

VI

All horses on the racecourse of Tralee
    Have four more legs in gallop than in trot—
    Two pairs fully extended, two pairs not;
And yet no thoroughbred with either three
    Or five legs but is mercilessly shot.
I watched a filly gnaw her fifth leg free,
Warned by a speaking mare since turned silentiary.

THE EUGENIST

Come, human dogs, interfertilitate—
  Blackfellow and white lord, brown, yellow and red!
Accept the challenge of the lately bred
  Newfoundland terrier with the dachshund gait.[1]

Breed me gigantic pygmies, meek-eyed Scots,
  Phlegmatic Irish, perfume-hating Poles,
Poker-faced, toothy, pigtailed Hottentots,
  And Germans with no envy in their souls.

[1] *See:* Charles R. Stockard and collaborators: *The genetic and
endocrinic basis for differences in form and behaviour, as eluci-
dated by studies of contrasted pure-line dogbreeds and their
hybrids.* (Philadelphia, 1941.)

A CIVIL SERVANT

While in this cavernous place employed
  Not once was I aware
Of my officious other-self
  Poised high above me there,

My self reversed, my rage-less part,
  A slimy yellowish cone—
Drip, drip; drip, drip—so down the years
  I stalagmized in stone.

Now pilgrims to the cave, who come
  To chip off what they can,
Prod me with child-like merriment:
  'Look, look! It's like a man!'

GULLS AND MEN

The naturalists of the Bass Rock
  On this vexatious point agree:
That sea-birds of all sorts that flock
  About the Bass, repeatedly
    Collide in mid-flight,

And neither by design, in play,
  Nor by design, in shrewd assault,
But (as these patient watchers say,
  Eyes that are seldom proved at fault)
    By lack of foresight.

Stupidity, which poor and rich
  Hold the recognizance of man,
Precious stupidity, of which
  Let him denude himself who can
    And stand at God's height—

Stupidity that brings to birth
  More, always more, than to the grave,
The burden of all songs on earth,
  And by which men are brave
    And women contrite—

This jewel bandied from a cliff
  By gulls and razor-bills and such!
Where is man's vindication if
  Perfectibility's as much
    Bird-right as man-right?

CONVERSATION PIECE

By moonlight
At midnight,
Under the vines,
A hotel chair
Settles down moodily before the headlines
Of a still-folded evening newspaper.

The other chair
Of the pair
Lies on its back,
Stiff as in pain,
Having been overturned with an angry crack;
And there till morning, alas, it must remain.

On the terrace
No blood-trace,
No sorry glitter
Of a knife, nothing:
Not even the fine-torn fragments of a letter
Or the dull gleam of a flung-off wedding-ring.

Still stable
On the table
Two long-stemmed glasses,
One full of drink,
Watch how the rat among the vines passes
And how the moon trembles on the crag's brink.

GENERAL BLOODSTOCK'S
LAMENT FOR ENGLAND

'This image (seemingly animated) walks with them in the
fields in broad Day-light; and if they are employed in delving,
harrowing, Seed-sowing or any other Occupation, they are at
the same time mimicked by the ghostly Visitant. Men of the
Second Sight . . . call this reflex-man a Co-walker, every way
like the Man, as his Twin-brother and Companion, haunting
as his Shadow.'   Kirk's *Secret Commonwealth*, 1691.

Alas, England, my own generous mother,
One gift I have from you I hate,
The second sight: I see your weird co-walker,
Silver-zoned Albion, stepping in your track,
Mimicking your sad and doubtful gait,
Your clasped hands, your head-shakings, your bent back.

The white hem of a winding sheet
Draws slowly upward from her feet;
Soon it will mount knee-high, then to the thigh.
It crackles like the parchment of the treaties,
Bonds, contracts and conveyances,
With which, beggared and faint and like to die,
You signed away your island sovereignty
To rogues who learned their primer at your knees.

'¡WELLCOME, TO THE CAVES OF ARTÁ!'

'They are hollowed out in the see coast at the muncipal ter-
minal of Capdepera, at nine kilometer from the town of Artá
in the Island of Mallorca, with a suporizing infinity of graceful
colums of 21 meter and by downward, wich prives the spec-
tator of all animacion and plunges in dumbness. The way going is very picturesque, serpentine between style mountains,
til the arrival at the esplanade of the vallee called "The
Spider". There are good enlacements of the railroad with auto-
buses of excursion, many days of the week, today actually
Wednesday and Satturday. Since many centuries renown fore-
ing visitors have explored them and wrote their eulogy about,
included Nort-American geoglogues.' *From a Tourist leaflet.*

Such subtile filigranity and nobless of construccion
  Here fraternise in harmony, that respiracion stops.
While all admit their impotence (though autors most formidable)
  To sing in words the excellence of Nature's underprops,
Yet stalactite and stalagmite together with dumb language
  Make hymnes to God wich celebrate the strength of water drops.

¿You, also, are you capable to make precise in idiom
  Consideracions magic of ilusions very wide?
Alraedy in the Vestibule of these Grand Caves of Artá
  The spirit of the human verb is darked and stupefyed;
So humildy you trespass trough the forest of the colums
  And listen to the grandess explicated by the guide.

From darkness into darkness, but at measure, now descending
  You remark with what esxactitude he designates each bent;
'The Saloon of Thousand Banners', or 'The Tumba of Napoleon',
  'The Grotto of the Rosary', 'The Club', 'The Camping Tent'.
And at 'Cavern of the Organ' there are knocking streange formacions
  Wich give a nois particular pervoking wonderment.

¡Too far do not adventure, sir! For, further as you wander,
  The every of the stalactites will make you stop and stay.
Grand peril amenaces now, your nostrills aprehending
  An odour least delicious of lamentable decay.
It is some poor touristers, in the depth of obscure cristal,
  Wich deceased of thier emocion on a past excursion day.

I'M THROUGH WITH YOU FOR EVER

The oddest, surely, of odd tales
    Recorded by the French
Concerns a sneak thief of Marseilles
    Tried by a callous Bench.

His youth, his innocency, his tears—
    No, nothing could abate
Their sentence of 'One hundred years
    In galleys of the State.'

Nevertheless, old wives affirm
    And annalists agree,
He sweated out the whole damned term,
    Bowed stiffly, and went free.

Then come, my angry love, review
    Your sentence of today.
'For ever' was unjust of you,
    The end too far away.

Give me four hundred years, or five—
    Can rage be so intense?—
And I will sweat them out alive
    To prove my impenitence.

THE SACRED MISSION

The ungainsayable, huge, cooing message
Hurtles suddenly down the dawn streets:
Twenty loudspeakers, twenty lovesick voices
Each zealous to enlarge his own range
And dominate the echoing border-zones.

Now the distressed whimper of little children,
The groans of sick men cheated in their hope
Of snatching a light sleep from the jaws of pain,
The curses, even, of the unregenerate—
All are submerged in the rising sea of noise
Which floods each room and laps round every pillow,
Roaring the mercy of Christ's limitless love.

POETS' CORNER

De ambobus mundis ille
Convoravit diligens . . .

The Best of Both Worlds being Got
Between th'Evangel and the Pot,
He, though Exorbitantly Vice'd,
Had Re-discover'd Thirst for Christ
And Fell a Victim (Young as This)
To Ale, God's Love and Syphilis.

Here then in Triumph See Him Stand,
Laurels for Halo, Scroll in Hand,
Whyle Ganymeds and Cherubim
And Squabby Nymphs Rejoyce with Him:
Aye, Scroll Shall Fall and Laurels Fade
Long, Long before his Debts are Pay'd.

BEAUTY IN TROUBLE

Beauty in trouble flees to the good angel
   On whom she can rely
To pay her cab-fare, run a steaming bath,
   Poultice her bruised eye;

Will not at first, whether for shame or caution,
   Her difficulty disclose;
Until he draws a cheque book from his plumage,
   Asking how much she owes.

(Breakfast in bed: coffee and marmalade,
   Toast, eggs, orange-juice,
After a long, sound sleep—the first since when?—
   And no word of abuse.)

Loves him less only than her saint-like mother,
   Promises to repay
His loans and most seraphic thoughtfulness
   A million-fold one day.

Beauty grows plump, renews her broken courage
   And, borrowing ink and pen,
Writes a news-letter to the evil angel
   (Her first gay act since when?):

The fiend who beats, betrays and sponges on her,
   Persuades her white is black,
Flaunts vespertilian wing and cloven hoof;
   And soon will fetch her back.

Virtue, good angel, is its own reward:
   Your guineas were well spent.
But would you to the marriage of true minds
   Admit impediment?

SIROCCO AT DEYÁ

How most unnatural-seeming, yet how proper;
The sea like a cat with fur rubbed the wrong way,
As the sirocco with its furnace flavour
Dashes at full tilt around the village
['From every-which-a-way, hot as a two-buck pistol']
Stripping green olives from the blown-back boughs,
Scorching the roses, blinding the eyes with sand;
While slanderous tongues in the small cafés
And in the tightly-shuttered granite houses
Clack defamation, incite and invite
Knives to consummate their near-murders . . .
Look up, a great grey cloud broods nonchalant
On the mountain-top nine hundred feet above us,
Motionless and turgid, blotting out the sun,
And from it sneers a supercilious Devil:
'Mere local wind: no messenger of mine!'

FROM THE EMBASSY

I, an ambassador of Otherwhere
To the unfederated states of Here and There
Enjoy (as the phrase is)
Extra-territorial privileges.
With heres and theres I seldom come to blows
Or need, as once, to sandbag all my windows.
And though the Otherwhereish currency
Cannot be quoted yet officially,
I meet less hindrance now with the exchange
Nor is my garb, even, considered strange;
And shy enquiries for literature
Come in by every post, and the side door.

VIII

THE WHITE GODDESS

All saints revile her, and all sober men
Ruled by the God Apollo's golden mean—
In scorn of which we sailed to find her
In distant regions likeliest to hold her
Whom we desired above all things to know,
Sister of the mirage and echo.

It was a virtue not to stay,
To go our headstrong and heroic way
Seeking her out at the volcano's head,
Among pack ice, or where the track had faded
Beyond the cavern of the seven sleepers:
Whose broad high brow was white as any leper's,
Whose eyes were blue, with rowan-berry lips,
With hair curled honey-coloured to white hips.

Green sap of Spring in the young wood a-stir
Will celebrate the Mountain Mother,
And every song-bird shout awhile for her;
But we are gifted, even in November
Rawest of seasons, with so huge a sense
Of her nakedly worn magnificence
We forget cruelty and past betrayal,
Heedless of where the next bright bolt may fall.

AMERGIN'S CHARM

[The text restored from mediaeval Irish and Welsh variants.]

I am a stag: *of seven tines,*
I am a flood: *across a plain,*
I am a wind: *on a deep lake,*
I am a tear: *the Sun lets fall,*
I am a hawk: *above the cliff,*
I am a thorn: *beneath the nail,*
I am a wonder: *among flowers,*
I am a wizard: *who but I*
Sets the cool head aflame with smoke?

I am a spear: *that roars for blood,*
I am a salmon: *in a pool,*
I am a lure: *from paradise,*
I am a hill: *where poets walk,*
I am a boar: *renowned and red,*
I am a breaker: *threatening doom,*
I am a tide: *that drags to death,*
I am an infant: *who but I*
Peeps from the unhewn dolmen arch?

I am the womb: *of every holt,*
I am the blaze: *on every hill,*
I am the queen: *of every hive,*
I am the shield: *for every head,*
I am the grave: *of every hope.*

THE BATTLE OF THE TREES

[Text reassembled and restored from the deliberately confused mediaeval Welsh poem-medley, *Câd Goddeu*, in the *Red Book of Hergest*, hitherto regarded as nonsensical.]

The tops of the beech tree
  Have sprouted of late,
Are changed and renewed
  From their withered state.

When the beech prospers,
  Though spells and litanies
The oak tops entangle,
  There is hope for trees.

I have plundered the fern,
  Through all secrets I spy,
Old Math ap Mathonwy
  Knew no more than I.

With nine sorts of faculty
  God has gifted me:
I am fruit of fruits gathered
  From nine sorts of tree—

Plum, quince, whortle, mulberry,
  Raspberry, pear,
Black cherry and white
  With the sorb in me share.

From my seat at Fefynedd,
  A city that is strong,
I watched the trees and green things
  Hastening along.

Retreating from happiness
  They would fain be set
In forms of the chief letters
  Of the alphabet.

Wayfarers wondered,
　Warriors were dismayed
At renewal of conflicts
　Such as Gwydion made,

Under the tongue root
　A fight most dread,
And another raging
　Behind, in the head.

The alders in the front line
　Began the affray.
Willow and rowan-tree
　Were tardy in array.

The holly, dark green,
　Made a resolute stand;
He is armed with many spear points
　Wounding the hand.

With foot-beat of the swift oak
　Heaven and earth rung;
'Stout Guardian of the Door',
　His name in every tongue.

Great was the gorse in battle,
　And the ivy at his prime;
The hazel was arbiter
　At this charmed time.

Uncouth and savage was the fir,
　Cruel the ash-tree—
Turns not aside a foot-breadth,
　Straight at the heart runs he.

The birch, though very noble,
   Armed himself but late:
A sign not of cowardice
   But of high estate.

The heath gave consolation
   To the toil-spent folk,
The long-enduring poplars
   In battle much broke.

Some of them were cast away
   On the field of fight
Because of holes torn in them
   By the enemy's might.

Very wrathful was the vine
   Whose henchmen are the elms;
I exalt him mightily
   To rulers of realms.

Strong chieftains were the blackthorn
   With his ill fruit,
The unbeloved whitethorn
   Who wears the same suit,

The swift-pursuing reed,
   The broom with his brood,
And the furze but ill-behaved
   Until he is subdued.

The dower-scattering yew
   Stood glum at the fight's fringe,
With the elder slow to burn
   Amid fires that singe,

And the blessed wild apple
   Laughing in pride
From the *Gorchan* of Maelderw
   By the rock side.

In shelter linger
   Privet and woodbine,
Inexperienced in warfare,
   And the courtly pine.

But I, although slighted
   Because I was not big,
Fought, trees, in your array
   On the field of Goddeu Brig.

THE SONG OF BLODEUWEDD

[Text reassembled and restored from the same poem-medley as the foregoing.]

Not of father nor of mother
Was my blood, was my body.
I was spellbound by Gwydion,
Prime enchanter of the Britons,
When he formed me from nine blossoms,
   Nine buds of various kind:
From primrose of the mountain,
Broom, meadow-street and cockle,
   Together intertwined,
From the bean in its shade bearing
A white spectral army
   Of earth, of earthy kind,
From blossoms of the nettle,
Oak, thorn and bashful chestnut—
Nine powers of nine flowers,
   Nine powers in me combined,
      Nine buds of plant and tree.
Long and white are my fingers
      As the ninth wave of the sea.

INSTRUCTIONS TO THE ORPHIC ADEPT

[In part translated from the *Timpone Grande* and *Campagno*
Orphic tablets.]

So soon as ever your mazed spirit descends
From daylight into darkness, Man, remember
What you have suffered here in Samothrace,
What you have suffered.

After your passage through Hell's seven floods,
Whose fumes of sulphur will have parched your throat,
The Halls of Judgement shall loom up before you,
A miracle of jasper and of onyx.
To the left hand there bubbles a black spring
Overshadowed with a great white cypress.
Avoid this spring, which is Forgetfulness;
Though all the common rout rush down to drink,
Avoid this spring!

To the right hand there lies a secret pool
Alive with speckled trout and fish of gold;
A hazel overshadows it. Ophion,
Primaeval serpent straggling in the branches,
Darts out his tongue. This holy pool is fed
By dripping water; guardians stand before it.
Run to this pool, the pool of Memory,
Run to this pool!

Then will the guardians scrutinize you, saying:
'Who are you, who? What have you to remember?
Do you not fear Ophion's flickering tongue?
Go rather to the spring beneath the cypress,
Flee from this pool!'

Then you shall answer: 'I am parched with thirst.
Give me to drink. I am a child of Earth,
But of Sky also, come from Samothrace.
Witness the glint of amber on my brow.
Out of the Pure I come, as you may see.

I also am of your thrice-blessèd kin,
Child of the three-fold Queen of Samothrace;
Have made full quittance for my deeds of blood,
Have been by her invested in sea-purple,
And like a kid have fallen into milk.
Give me to drink, now I am parched with thirst,
Give me to drink!'

But they will ask you yet: 'What of your feet?'
You shall reply: 'My feet have borne me here
Out of the weary wheel, the circling years,
To that still, spokeless wheel:—Persephone.
Give me to drink!'

Then they will welcome you with fruit and flowers,
And lead you toward the ancient dripping hazel,
Crying: 'Brother of our immortal blood,
Drink and remember glorious Samothrace!'
Then you shall drink.

You shall drink deep of that refreshing draught,
To become lords of the uninitiated
Twittering ghosts, Hell's countless populace—
To become heroes, knights upon swift horses,
Pronouncing oracles from tall white tombs
By the nymphs tended. They with honey water
Shall pour libations to your serpent shapes,
That you may drink.

LAMENT FOR PASIPHAË

Dying sun, shine warm a little longer!
My eye, dazzled with tears, shall dazzle yours,
Conjuring you to shine and not to move.
You, sun, and I all afternoon have laboured
Beneath a dewless and oppressive cloud—
A fleece now gilded with our common grief
That this must be a night without a moon.
Dying sun, shine warm a little longer!

Faithless she was not: she was very woman,
Smiling with dire impartiality,
Sovereign, with heart unmatched, adored of men,
Until Spring's cuckoo with bedraggled plumes
Tempted her pity and her truth betrayed.
Then she who shone for all resigned her being,
And this must be a night without a moon.
Dying sun, shine warm a little longer!

THE SIRENS' WELCOME TO CRONOS

Cronos the Ruddy, steer your boat
Toward Silver Island whence we sing;
Here you shall pass your days.

Through a thick-growing alder-wood
We clearly see, but are not seen,
Hid in a golden haze.

Our hair the hue of barley sheaf,
Our eyes the hue of blackbird's egg
Our cheeks like asphodel.

Here the wild apple blossoms yet;
Wrens in the silver branches play
And prophesy you well.

Here nothing ill or harsh is found.
Cronos the Ruddy, steer your boat
Across these placid straits,

With each of us in turn to lie
Taking your pleasure on young grass
That for your coming waits.

No grief nor gloom, sickness nor death,
Disturbs our long tranquillity;
No treachery, no greed.

Compared with this, what are the plains
Of Elis, where you ruled as king?
A wilderness indeed.

A starry crown awaits your head,
A hero feast is spread for you:
Swineflesh, milk and mead.

INTERCESSION IN LATE OCTOBER

How hard the year dies: no frost yet.
On drifts of yellow sand Midas reclines,
Fearless of moaning reed or sullen wave.
Firm and fragrant still the brambleberries.
On ivy-bloom butterflies wag.

Spare him a little longer, Crone,
For his clean hands and love-submissive heart.

THE JACKALS' ADDRESS TO ISIS

Grant Anup's children this:
To howl with you, Queen Isis,
Over the scattered limbs of wronged Osiris.
What harder fate than to be woman?
She makes and she unmakes her man.
In Jackal-land it is no secret
Who tempted red-haired, ass-eared Set
To such bloody extreme; who most
Must therefore mourn and fret
To pacify the unquiet ghost.
And when Horus your son
Avenges this divulsion,
Sceptre in fist, sandals on feet,
We shall return across the sand
From loyal Jackal-land
To gorge five nights and days on ass's meat.

THE DESTROYER

Swordsman of the narrow lips,
Narrow hips and murderous mind
Fenced with chariots and ships,
By your joculators hailed
The mailed wonder of mankind,
Far to westward you have sailed.

You it was dared seize the throne
Of a blown and amorous prince
Destined to the Moon alone,
A lame, golden-heeled decoy,
Joy of hens that gape and wince
Inarticulately coy.

You who, capped with lunar gold
Like an old and savage dunce,
Let the central hearth go cold,
Grinned, and left us here your sword
Warden of sick fields that once
Sprouted of their own accord.

Gusts of laughter the Moon stir
That her Bassarids now bed
With the ignoble usurer
While an ignorant pale priest
Rides the beast with a man's head
To her long-omitted feast.

RETURN OF THE GODDESS

Under your Milky Way
  And slow-revolving Bear
Frogs from the alder thicket pray
In terror of your judgement day,
  Loud with repentance there.

The log they crowned as king
  Grew sodden, lurched and sank;
An owl floats by on silent wing,
Dark water bubbles from the spring;
  They invoke you from each bank.

At dawn you shall appear,
  A gaunt red-leggèd crane,
You whom they know too well for fear,
Lunging your beak down like a spear
  To fetch them home again.

> *Sufficiunt*
> *Tecum,*
> *Caryatis,*
> *Domnia*
> *Quina.*

IX

COUNTING THE BEATS

You, love, and I,
(He whispers) you and I,
And if no more than only you and I
What care you or I?

Counting the beats,
Counting the slow heart beats,
The bleeding to death of time in slow heart beats,
Wakeful they lie.

Cloudless day,
Night, and a cloudless day,
Yet the huge storm will burst upon their heads one day
From a bitter sky.

Where shall we be,
(She whispers) where shall we be,
When death strikes home, O where then shall we be
Who were you and I?

Not there but here,
(He whispers) only here,
As we are, here, together, now and here,
Always you and I.

Counting the beats,
Counting the slow heart beats,
The bleeding to death of time in slow heart beats,
Wakeful they lie.

THE YOUNG CORDWAINER

SHE: Love, why have you led me here
    To this lampless hall,
  A place of despair and fear
    Where blind things crawl?

HE: Not I, but your complaint
    Heard by the riverside
  That primrose scent grew faint
    And desire died.

SHE: Kisses had lost virtue
    As yourself must know;
  I declared what, alas, was true
    And still shall do so.

HE: Mount, sweetheart, this main stair
    Where bandogs at the foot
  Their crooked gilt teeth bare
    Between jaws of soot.

SHE: I loathe them, how they stand
    Like prick-eared spies.
  Hold me fast by the left hand;
    I walk with closed eyes.

HE: Primrose has periwinkle
    As her mortal fellow:
  Five leaves, blue and baleful,
    Five of true yellow.

SHE: Overhead, what's overhead?
    Where would you take me?
  My feet stumble for dread,
    My wits forsake me.

HE: Flight on flight, floor above floor,
    In suspense of doom
  To a locked secret door
    And a white-walled room.

SHE: Love, have you the pass-word,
    Or have you the key,
With a sharp naked sword
    And wine to revive me?

HE: Enter: here is starlight,
    Here the state bed
Where your man lies all night
    With blue flowers garlanded.

SHE: Ah, the cool open window
    Of this confessional!
With wine at my elbow,
And sword beneath the pillow,
    I shall perfect all.

YOUR PRIVATE WAY

Whether it was your way of walking
Or of laughing moved me,
At sight of you a song wavered
Ghostly on my lips; I could not voice it,
Uncertain what the notes or key.

Be thankful I am no musician,
Sweet Anonymity, to madden you
With your own private walking-laughing way
Imitated on a beggar's fiddle
Or blared across the square on All Fools' Day.

THE SURVIVOR

To die with a forlorn hope, but soon to be raised
By hags, the spoilers of the field, to elude their claws
And stand once more on a well-swept parade-ground,
Scarred and bemedalled, sword upright in fist
At head of a new undaunted company:

Is this joy?—to be doubtless alive again,
And the others dead? Will your nostrils gladly savour
The fragrance, always new, of a first hedge-rose?
Will your ears be charmed by the thrush's melody
Sung as though he had himself devised it?

And is this joy: after the double suicide
(Heart against heart) to be restored entire,
To smooth your hair and wash away the life-blood,
And presently seek a young and innocent bride.
Whispering in the dark: 'for ever and ever'?

QUESTIONS IN A WOOD

The parson to his pallid spouse,
  The hangman to his whore,
Do both not mumble the same vows,
  Both knock at the same door?

And when the fury of their knocks
  Has waned, and that was that,
What answer comes, unless the pox
  Or one more parson's brat?

Tell me, my love, my flower of flowers,
  True woman to this man,
What have their deeds to do with ours
  Or any we might plan?

Your startled gaze, your restless hand,
  Your hair like Thames in flood,
And choked voice, battling to command
  The insurgence of your blood:

How can they spell the dark word said
  Ten thousand times a night
By women as corrupt and dead
  As you are proud and bright?

And how can I, in the same breath,
  Though warned against the cheat,
Vilely deliver love to death
  Wrapped in a rumpled sheet?

Yet, if from delicacy of pride
  We choose to hold apart,
Will no blue hag appear, to ride
  Hell's wager in each heart?

DARIEN

It is a poet's privilege and fate
To fall enamoured of the one Muse
Who variously haunts this island earth.

She was your mother, Darien,
And presaged by the darting halcyon bird
Would run green-sleeved along her ridges,
Treading the asphodels and heather-trees
With white feet bare.

Often at moonrise I had watched her go
And a cold shudder shook me
To see the curved blaze of her Cretan axe.
Averted her set face, her business
Not yet with me, long-striding,
She would ascend the peak and pass from sight.
But once at full moon, by the sea's verge,
I came upon her without warning.

Unrayed she stood, with long hair streaming,
A cockle-shell cupped in her warm hands,
Her axe propped idly on a stone.

No awe possessed me, only a great grief;
Wanly she smiled, but would not lift her eyes
(As a young girl will greet the stranger).
I stood upright, a head taller than she.
'See who has come,' said I.

She answered: 'If I lift my eyes to yours
And our eyes marry, man, what then?
Will they engender my son Darien?
Swifter than wind, with straight and nut-brown hair,
Tall, slender-shanked, grey-eyed, untameable;
Never was born, nor ever will be born
A child to equal my son Darien,
Guardian of the hid treasures of your world.'

I knew then by the trembling of her hands
For whom that flawless blade would sweep:
My own oracular head, swung by its hair.

'Mistress,' I cried, 'the times are evil
And you have charged me with their remedy.
O, where my head is now, let nothing be
But a clay counterfeit with nacre blink:
Only look up, so Darien may be born!

'He is the northern star, the spell of knowledge,
Pride of all hunters and all fishermen,
Your deathless fawn, an eaglet of your eyrie,
The topmost branch of your unfellable tree,
A tear streaking the summer night,
The new green of my hope.'
                                        Lifting her eyes,
She held mine for a lost eternity.
'Sweetheart,' said I, 'strike now, for Darien's sake!'

THE PORTRAIT

She speaks always in her own voice
Even to strangers; but those other women
Exercise their borrowed, or false, voices
Even on sons and daughters.

She can walk invisibly at noon
Along the high road; but those other women
Gleam phosphorescent—broad hips and gross fingers—
Down every lampless alley.

She is wild and innocent, pledged to love
Through all disaster; but those other women
Decry her for a witch or a common drab
And glare back when she greets them.

Here is her portrait, gazing sidelong at me,
The hair in disarray, the young eyes pleading:
'And you, love? As unlike those other men
As I those other women?'

PROMETHEUS

Close bound in a familiar bed
All night I tossed, rolling my head;
Now dawn returns in vain, for still
The vulture squats on her warm hill.

I am in love as giants are
That dote upon the evening star,
And this lank bird is come to prove
The intractability of love.

Yet still, with greedy eye half shut,
Rend the raw liver from its gut:
Feed, jealousy, do not fly away—
If she who fetched you also stay.

THE STRAW

Peace, the wild valley streaked with torrents,
A hoopoe perched on his warm rock. Then why
This tremor of the straw between my fingers?

What should I fear? Have I not testimony
In her own hand, signed with her own name
That my love fell as lightning on her heart?

These questions, bird, are not rhetorical.
Watch how the straw twitches and leaps
As though the earth quaked at a distance.

Requited love; but better unrequited
If this chance instrument gives warning
Of cataclysmic anguish far away.

Were she at ease, warmed by the thought of me,
Would not my hand stay steady as this rock?
Have I undone her by my vehemence?

CRY FAUGH!

Caria and Philistia considered
Only pre-marital adventures wise;
The bourgeois French argue contrariwise.

Socrates and Plato burked the issue
(Namely, how man-and-woman love should be)
With homosexual ideology.

Apocalyptic Israelites, foretelling
The Imminent End, called only for a chaste
Sodality: all dead below the waist.

Curious, various, amoral, moral—
Confess, what elegant square or lumpish hamlet
Lives free from nymphological disquiet?

'Yet males and females of the lower species
Contrive to eliminate the sexual problem,'
Scientists ponder: 'Why not learn from them?'

Cry faugh! on science, ethics, metaphysics,
On antonyms of sacred and profane—
Come walk with me, love, in a golden rain

Past toppling colonnades of glory,
The moon alive on each uptilted face:
Proud remnants of a visionary race.

HERCULES AT NEMEA

Muse, you have bitten through my fool's-finger.
Maned like a lioness you held it
In your white teeth most amorously;
And I stared back, dauntless and fiery-eyed,
Challenging you to maim me for my pride.

See me a fulvous hero of nine fingers—
Sufficient grasp for bow and arrow.
My beard bristles in exultation:
Let all Nemea look and understand
Why you have set your mark on this right hand.

DIALOGUE ON THE HEADLAND

SHE: You'll not forget these rocks and what I told you?

HE: How could I? Never: whatever happens.

SHE: What do you think might happen?
Might you fall out of love?—did you mean that?

HE: Never, never! 'Whatever' was a sop
For jealous listeners in the shadows.

SHE: You haven't answered me. I asked:
'What do you think might happen?'

HE: Whatever happens: though the skies should fall
Raining their larks and vultures in our laps—

SHE: 'Though the seas turn to slime'—say that—
'Though water-snakes be hatched with six heads.'

HE: Though the seas turn to slime, or tower
In an arching wave above us, three miles high—

SHE: 'Though she should break with you',—dare you say that?—
'Though she deny her words on oath.'

HE: I had that in my mind to say, or nearly;
It hurt so much I choked it back.

SHE: How many other days can't you forget?
How many other loves and landscapes?

HE: You are jealous?

SHE: Damnably.

HE: The past is past.

SHE: And this?

HE: Whatever happens, this goes on.

SHE: Without a future? Sweetheart, tell me now:
What do you want of me? I must know that.

HE: Nothing that isn't freely mine already.

SHE: Say what is freely yours and you shall have it.

HE: Nothing that, loving you, I could dare take.

SHE: O, for an answer with no 'nothing' in it!

HE: Then give me everything that's left.

SHE: Left after what?

HE: After whatever happens:
Skies have already fallen, seas are slime,
Watersnakes poke and peer six-headedly—

SHE: And I lie snugly in the Devil's arms.

HE: I said: 'Whatever happens.' Are you crying?

SHE: You'll not forget me—ever, ever, ever?

THE MARK

If, doubtful of your fate,
You seek to obliterate
And to forget
The counter-mark I set
In the warm blue-veined nook
Of your elbow crook,
How can you not repent
The experiment?

No knife nor fang went in
To lacerate the skin;
Nor may the eye
Tetter or wen descry:
The place which my lips pressed
Is coloured like the rest
And fed by the same blood
Of womanhood.

Acid, pumice-stone,
Lancings to the bone,
Would be in vain.
Here must the mark remain
As witness to such love
As nothing can remove
Or blur, or hide,
Save suicide.

LIADAN AND CURITHIR

Even in childhood
Liadan never would
  Accept love simply,
But stifled longing
And went away to sing
  In strange company.

Alas, for Liadan!
To fear perfection
  Was her ill custom:
Choosing a scruple
That might seem honourable,
  For retreat therefrom.

Herself she enticed
To be nunned for Christ,
  Though in marriage sought
By a master-poet
On whom her heart was set—
  Curithir of Connaught;

And raised a wall
As it were of crystal
  Her grief around.
He might not guess
The cause of her fickleness
  Nor catch one sound.

She was walled soon after
Behind stones and mortar,
  From whence too late
He heard her keening,
Sighing and complaining
  Of her dire self-hate.

THE SEA HORSE

Since now in every public place
Lurk phantoms who assume your walk and face,
You cannot yet have utterly abjured me
Nor stifled the insistent roar of sea.

Do as I do: confide your unquiet love
(For one who never owed you less than love)
To this indomitable hippocamp,
Child of your element, coiled a-ramp,
Having ridden out worse tempests than you know of;
Under his horny ribs a blood-red stain
Portends renewal of our pain.
Sweetheart, make much of him and shed
Tears on his taciturn dry head.

REPROACH TO JULIA

Julia: how Irishly you sacrifice
Love to pity, pity to ill-humour,
Yourself to love, still haggling at the price.

DETHRONEMENT

With pain pressing so close about your heart,
Stand (it behoves you), head uncovered,
To watch how she enacts her transformations—
Bitch, vixen, sow—the laughing, naked queen
Who has now dethroned you.

Hymns to her beauty or to her mercy
Would be ill-conceived. Your true anguish
Is all that she requires. You, turned to stone,
May not speak nor groan, shall stare dumbly,
Grinning dismay.

But as the play ends, or in its after-hush,
O then, deluded, flee! Her red-eared hounds
Scramble upon your track; past either cheek
Swan-feathered arrows whistle, or cruelly comb
Long furrows in your scalp.

Run, though you hope for nothing: to stay your foot
Would be ingratitude, a sour denial
That the life she bestowed was sweet.
Therefore be fleet, run gasping, draw the chase
Up the grand defile.

They will rend you to rags assuredly
With half a hundred love-bites—
Your hot blood an acceptable libation
Poured to Persephone, in whose domain
You shall again find peace.

CAT-GODDESSES

A perverse habit of cat-goddesses—
Even the blackest of them, black as coals
Save for a new moon blazing on each breast,
With coral tongues and beryl eyes like lamps,
Long-leggèd, pacing three by three in nines—
This obstinate habit is to yield themselves,
In verisimilar love-ecstasies,
To tatter-eared and slinking alley-toms
No less below the common run of cats
Than they above it; which they do for spite,
To provoke jealousy—not the least abashed
By such gross-headed, rabbit-coloured litters
As soon they shall be happy to desert.

THE BLUE-FLY

Five summer days, five summer nights,
The ignorant, loutish, giddy blue-fly
Hung without motion on the cling peach,
Humming occasionally: 'O my love, my fair one!'
    As in the *Canticles*.

Magnified one thousand times, the insect
Looks farcically human; laugh if you will!
Bald head, stage-fairy wings, blear eyes,
A caved-in chest, hairy black mandibles,
    Long spindly thighs.

The crime was detected on the sixth day.
What then could be said or done? By anyone?
It would have been vindictive, mean and what-not
To swat that fly for being a blue-fly,
    For debauch of a peach.

Is it fair, either, to bring a microscope
To bear on the case, even in search of truth?
Nature, doubtless, has some compelling cause
To glut the carriers of her epidemics—
    Nor did the peach complain.

A LOST JEWEL

Who on your breast pillows his head now,
Jubilant to have won
The heart beneath on fire for him alone,

At dawn will hear you, plagued by nightmare,
Mumble and weep
About some blue jewel you were sworn to keep.

Wake, blink, laugh out in reassurance,
Yet your tears will say:
'It was not mine to lose or give away.

'For love it shone—never for the madness
Of a strange bed—
Light on my finger, fortune in my head.'

Roused by your naked grief and beauty,
For lust he will burn:
'Turn to me, sweetheart! Why do you not turn?'

THE WINDOW SILL

Presage and caveat not only seem
To come in dream,
But do so come in dream.

When the cock crew and phantoms floated by,
This dreamer I
Out of the house went I,

Down long unsteady streets to a queer square;
And who was there,
Or whom did I know there?

Julia, leaning on her window sill.
'I love you still,'
She said, 'O love me still!'

I answered: 'Julia, do you love me best?'
'What of this breast,'
She mourned, 'this flowery breast?'

Then a wild sobbing spread from door to door,
And every floor
Cried shame on every floor,

As she unlaced her bosom to disclose
Each breast a rose,
A white and cankered rose.

SPOILS

When all is over and you march for home,
The spoils of war are easily disposed of:
Standards, weapons of combat, helmets, drums
May decorate a staircase or a study,
While lesser gleanings of the battlefield—
Coins, watches, wedding-rings, gold teeth and such—
Are sold anonymously for solid cash.

The spoils of love present a different case,
When all is over and you march for home:
That lock of hair, these letters and the portrait
May not be publicly displayed; nor sold;
Nor burned; nor returned (the heart being obstinate)—
Yet never dare entrust them to a safe
For fear they burn a hole through two-foot steel.

RHEA

On her shut lids the lightning flickers,
Thunder explodes above her bed,
An inch from her lax arm the rain hisses;
Discrete she lies,

Not dead but entranced, dreamlessly
With slow breathing, her lips curved
In a half-smile archaic, her breast bare,
Hair astream.

The house rocks, a flood suddenly rising
Bears away bridges: oak and ash
Are shivered to the roots—royal green timber.
She nothing cares.

(Divine Augustus, trembling at the storm,
Wrapped sealskin on his thumb; divine Gaius
Made haste to hide himself in a deep cellar,
Distraught by fear.)

Rain, thunder, lightning: pretty children.
'Let them play,' her mother-mind repeats;
'They do no harm, unless from high spirits
Or by mishap.'

X

THE FACE IN THE MIRROR

Grey haunted eyes, absent-mindedly glaring
From wide, uneven orbits; one brow drooping
Somewhat over the eye
Because of a missile fragment still inhering,
Skin-deep, as a foolish record of old-world fighting.

Crookedly broken nose—low tackling caused it;
Cheeks, furrowed; coarse grey hair, flying frenetic;
Forehead, wrinkled and high;
Jowls, prominent; ears, large; jaw, pugilistic;
Teeth, few; lips, full and ruddy; mouth, ascetic.

I pause with razor poised, scowling derision
At the mirrored man whose beard needs my attention,
And once more ask him why
He still stands ready, with a boy's presumption,
To court the queen in her high silk pavilion.

THE CORAL POOL

It was a hippocamp addressed her darling,
   Perched on the coral branches of a pool
Where light reflected back from violet moss
   And fishes veered above in a tight school:

'Daughter, no sea is deep enough for drowning;
   Therefore let none seem broad enough for you,
My foal, my fledgeling bird, my dragon-imp,
   Or understand a tithe of what you do.

'To wanton fish never divulge your secret,
   But only to our mistress of the tides
Whose handy-men are octopus and crab,
   At whose white heel the amorous turtle glides.'

GRATITUDE FOR A NIGHTMARE

His appearances are incalculable,
His strength terrible,
I do not know his name.

Huddling pensive for weeks on end, he
Gives only random hints of life, such as
Strokes of uncomfortable coincidence.

To eat heartily, dress warmly, lie snugly
And earn respect as a leading citizen
Granted long credit at all shops and inns—

How dangerous! I had feared this shag demon
Would not conform with my conformity
And in some leaner belly make his lair.

But now in dream he suddenly bestrides me . . .
'All's well,' I groan, and fumble for a light,
Brow bathed in sweat, heart pounding.

FRIDAY NIGHT

Love, the sole Goddess fit for swearing by,
Concedes us graciously the little lie:
The white lie, the half-lie, the lie corrective
Without which love's exchange might prove defective,
Confirming hazardous relationships
By kindly *maquillage* of Truth's pale lips.

This little lie was first told, so they say,
On the sixth day (Love's planetary day)
When, meeting her full-bosomed and half dressed,
Jove roared out suddenly: 'Hell take the rest!
Six hard days of Creation are enough'—
And clasped her to him, meeting no rebuff.

Next day he rested, and she rested too.
The busy little lie between them flew:
'If this be not perfection,' Love would sigh,
'Perfection is a great, black, thumping lie . . .'
Endearments, kisses, grunts, and whispered oaths;
But were her thoughts on breakfast, or on clothes?

THE NAKED AND THE NUDE

For me, the naked and the nude
(By lexicographers construed
As synonyms that should express
The same deficiency of dress
Or shelter) stand as wide apart
As love from lies, or truth from art.

Lovers without reproach will gaze
On bodies naked and ablaze;
The Hippocratic eye will see
In nakedness, anatomy;
And naked shines the Goddess when
She mounts her lion among men.

The nude are bold, the nude are sly
To hold each treasonable eye.
While draping by a showman's trick
Their dishabille in rhetoric,
They grin a mock-religious grin
Of scorn at those of naked skin.

The naked, therefore, who compete
Against the nude may know defeat;
Yet when they both together tread
The briary pastures of the dead,
By Gorgons with long whips pursued,
How naked go the sometime nude!

WOMAN AND TREE

To love one woman, or to sit
   Always beneath the same tall tree,
Argues a certain lack of wit
   Two steps from imbecility.

A poet, therefore, sworn to feed
   On every food the senses know,
Will claim the inexorable need
   To be Don Juan Tenorio.

Yet if, miraculously enough,
   (And why set miracles apart?)
Woman and tree prove of a stuff
   Wholly to glamour his wild heart?

And if such visions from the void
   As shone in fever there, or there,
Assemble, hold and are enjoyed
   On climbing one familiar stair . . . ?

To change and chance he took a vow,
   As he thought fitting. None the less,
What of a phoenix on the bough,
   Or a sole woman's fatefulness?

FORBIDDEN WORDS

There are some words carry a curse with them:
Smooth-trodden, abstract, slippery vocables.
They beckon like a path of stepping stones;
But lift them up and watch what writhes or scurries!

Concepts barred from the close language of love—
Darling, you use no single word of the list,
Unless ironically in truth's defence
To volley it back against the abstractionist.

Which is among your several holds on my heart;
For you are no uninstructed child of Nature,
But passed in schools and attained the laurel wreath:
Only to trample it on Apollo's floor.

A SLICE OF WEDDING CAKE

Why have such scores of lovely, gifted girls
   Married impossible men?
Simple self-sacrifice may be ruled out,
   And missionary endeavour, nine times out of ten.

Repeat 'impossible men': not merely rustic,
   Foul-tempered or depraved
(Dramatic foils chosen to show the world
   How well women behave, and always have behaved).

Impossible men: idle, illiterate,
   Self-pitying, dirty, sly,
For whose appearance even in City parks
   Excuses must be made to casual passers-by.

Has God's supply of tolerable husbands
   Fallen, in fact, so low?
Or do I always over-value woman
   At the expense of man?
                Do I?
                     It might be so.

A PLEA TO BOYS AND GIRLS

You learned Lear's *Nonsense Rhymes* by heart, not rote;
   You learned Pope's *Iliad* by rote, not heart;
These terms should be distinguished if you quote
   My verses, children—keep them poles apart—
And call the man a liar who says I wrote
   All that I wrote in love, for love of art.

NOTHING

NOTHING is circular,
Like the empty centre
Of a smoke-ring's shadow:
That colourless zero
Marked on a bare wall—
Nothing at all
And reflected in a mirror.

Then need you wonder
If the trained philosopher
Who seeks to define NOTHING
As absence of anything,
A world more logistically
Than, above, I
(Though my terms are cosier),

And claims he has found
That NOTHING is not round
Or hardly ever,
Will run a brain-fever
To the precise degree
Of one hundred and three
On Fahrenheit's thermometer?

CALL IT A GOOD MARRIAGE

Call it a good marriage—
For no one ever questioned
Her warmth, his masculinity,
Their interlocking views;
Except one stray graphologist
Who frowned in speculation
At her h's and her s's,
His p's and w's.

Though few would still subscribe
To the monogamic axiom
That strife below the hip-bones
Need not estrange the heart,
Call it a good marriage:
More drew those two together,
Despite a lack of children,
Than pulled them apart.

Call it a good marriage:
They never fought in public,
They acted circumspectly
And faced the world with pride;
Thus the hazards of their love-bed
Were none of our damned business—
Till as jurymen we sat on
Two deaths by suicide.

THE SECOND-FATED

My stutter, my cough, my unfinished sentences,
Denote an inveterate physical reluctance
To use the metaphysical idiom.
Forgive me: what I am saying is, perhaps, this:—

Your accepted universe, by Jove's naked hand
Or Esmun's, or Odomankoma's, or Marduk's—
Choose which name jibes—formed scientifically
From whatever there was before Time was,
And begging the question of perfect consequence,
May satisfy the general run of men
(If 'run' be an apt term for patent paralytics)
That blueprints destine all they suffer here,
But does not satisfy certain few else.

Fortune enrolled me among the second-fated
Who have read their own obituaries in *The Times*,
Have heard 'Where, death, thy sting? Where, grave, thy victory?'
Intoned with unction over their still clay,
Have seen two parallel red-ink lines drawn
Under their manic-depressive bank accounts,
And are therefore strictly forbidden to walk in grave-yards
Lest they scandalise the sexton and his bride.

We, to be plain with you, taking advantage
Of a brief demise, visited first the Pit,
A library of shades, completed characters;
And next the silver-bright Hyperborean Queendom,
Basking under the sceptre of Guess Whom?
Where pure souls matrilineally foregather.
We were then shot through by merciful lunar shafts
Until hearts tingled, heads sang, and praises flowed;
And learned to scorn your factitious universe
Ruled by the death which we had flouted;
Acknowledging only that from the Dove's egg hatched
Before aught was, but wind—unpredictable
As our second birth would be, or our second love:
A moon-warmed world of discontinuance.

THE TWIN OF SLEEP

Death is the twin of Sleep, they say:
   For I shall rise renewed,
Free from the cramps of yesterday,
   Clear-eyed and supple-thewed.

But though this bland analogy
   Helps other folk to face
Decrepitude, senility,
   Madness, disease, disgrace,

I do not like Death's greedy looks:
   Give me his twin instead—
Sleep never auctions off my books,
   My boots, my shirts, my bed.

AROUND THE MOUNTAIN

Some of you may know, others perhaps can guess
   How it is to walk all night through summer rain
(Thin rain that shrouds a beneficent full moon),
   To circle a mountain, and then limp home again.

The experience varies with a traveller's age
   And bodily strength, and strength of the love affair
That harries him out of doors in steady drizzle,
   With neither jacket nor hat, and holds him there.

Still, let us concede some common elements:
   Wild-fire that, until midnight, burns his feet;
And surging rankly up, strong on the palate,
   Scents of July, imprisoned by long heat.

Add: the sub-human, black tree-silhouettes
   Against a featureless pale pall of sky;
Unseen, gurgling water; the bulk and menace
   Of entranced houses; a wraith wandering by.

Milestones, each one witness of a new mood—
   Anger, desperation, grief, regret;
Her too-familiar face that whirls and totters
   In memory, never willing to stay set.

Whoever makes the desired turning-point,
   Which means another fifteen miles to go,
Learns more from dawn than love, so far, has taught him:
   Especially the false dawn, when cocks first crow.

Those last few miles are easy: being assured
   Of the truth, why should he fabricate fresh lies?
His house looms up; the eaves drip drowsily;
   The windows blaze to a resolute sunrise.

XI

LYCEIA

All the wolves of the forest
Howl for Lyceia,
Crowding together
In a close circle,
Tongues a-loll.

A silver serpent
Coiled at her waist
And a quiver at knee,
She combs fine tresses
With a fine comb:

Wolf-like, woman-like,
Gazing about her,
Greeting the wolves;
Partial to many,
Yet masked in pride.

The young wolves snarl,
They snap at one another
Under the moon.
'Beasts, be reasonable,
My beauty is my own!'

Lyceia has a light foot
For a weaving walk.
Her archer muscles
Warn them how tightly
She can stretch the string.

I question Lyceia,
Whom I find posted
Under the pine trees
One early morning:
'What do the wolves learn?'

'They learn only envy,'
Lyceia answers,
'Envy and hope,
Hope and chagrin.
Would you howl too
In that wolfish circle?'
She laughs as she speaks.

SYMPTOMS OF LOVE

Love is a universal migraine,
A bright stain on the vision,
Blotting out reason.

Symptoms of true love
Are leanness, jealousy,
Laggard dawns;

Are omens and nightmares—
Listening for a knock,
Waiting for a sign:

For a touch of her fingers
In a darkened room,
For a searching look.

Take courage, lover!
Could you endure such grief
At any hand but hers?

THE SHARP RIDGE

Since now I dare not ask
Any gift from you, or gentle task,
Or lover's promise—nor yet refuse
Whatever I can give and you dare choose—
Have pity on us both: choose well
On this sharp ridge dividing death from hell.

UNDER THE OLIVES

We never would have loved had love not struck
Swifter than reason, and despite reason:
Under the olives, our hands interlocked,
We both fell silent:
Each listened for the other's answering
Sigh of unreasonableness—
Innocent, gentle, bold, enduring, proud.

THE VISITATION

Drowsing in my chair of disbelief
I watch the door as it slowly opens—
A trick of the night wind?

Your slender body seems a shaft of moonlight
Against the door as it gently closes.
Do you cast no shadow?

Your whisper is too soft for credence,
Your tread like blossom drifting from a bough,
Your touch even softer.

You wear that sorrowful and tender mask
Which on high mountain tops in heather-flow
Entrances lonely shepherds;

And though a single word scatters all doubts,
I quake for wonder at your choice of me:
Why, why and why?

FRAGMENT

Are you shaken, are you stirred
By a whisper of love?
Spell-bound to a word
Does Time cease to move,
Till her calm grey eye
Expands to a sky
And the clouds of her hair
Like storms go by?

APPLE ISLAND

Though cruel seas like mountains fill the bay,
Wrecking the quayside huts,
Salting our vineyards with tall showers of spray;

And though the moon shines dangerously clear,
Fixed in another cycle
Than the sun's progress round the felloe'd year;

And though I may not hope to dwell apart
With you on Apple Island
Unless my breast be docile to the dart—

Why should I fear your element, the sea,
Or the full moon, your mirror,
Or the halved apple from your holy tree?

THE FALCON WOMAN

It is hard to be a man
Whose word is his bond
In love with such a woman,

When he builds on a promise
She lightly let fall
In carelessness of spirit.

The more sternly he asks her
To stand by that promise
The faster she flies.

But is it less hard
To be born such a woman
With wings like a falcon
And in carelessness of spirit
To love such a man?

TROUGHS OF SEA

'Do you delude yourself?' a neighbour asks,
Dismayed by my abstraction.
But though love cannot question love
Nor need deny its need,

Pity the man who finds a rebel heart
Under his breastbone drumming
Which reason warns him he should drown
In midnight wastes of sea.

Now as he stalks between tormented pines
(The moon in her last quarter)
A lissom spectre glides ahead
And utters not a word.

Waves, tasselled with dark weed come rearing up
Like castle waves, disclosing
Deep in their troughs a ribbed sea-floor
To break his bones upon.

—Clasp both your hands under my naked foot
And press hard, as I taught you:
A trick to mitigate the pangs
Either of birth or love.

THE LAUGH

Your sudden laugh restored felicity—
Everything grew clear that before would not:
The impossible genies, the extravagants,
Swung in to establish themselves fairly
As at last manageable elements
In a most daylight-simple plot.
It was the identity of opposites
Had so confused my all too sober wits.

THE DEATH GRAPPLE

Lying below your sheets, I challenge
A watersnake in a swoln cataract
Or a starved lioness among drifts of snow.

Yet dare it out, for after each death grapple,
Each gorgon stare borrowed from very hate,
A childish innocent smile touches your lips,
Your eyelids droop, fearless and careless,
And sleep remoulds the lineaments of love.

IN SINGLE SYLLABLES

Since I was with you last, at one with you,
Twelve hours have passed. Can I now swear it true
That love rose up in wrath to make us blind,
And stripped from us all powers of heart and mind,
So we were mad and had no pulse or thought
But love, love, love, in the one bale-fire caught?

You pass, you smile: yet is that smile I see
Of love, and of your all-night gift to me?
Now I too smile, for doubt, and own the doubt,
And wait in fear for night to root it out,
And doubt the more; but take heart to be true,
Each time of change, to a fresh hope of you,
That love may prove his worth once more and be
Fierce as the tides of Spring in you and me,
And bear with us till dawn shall break, though soon
With dreams of doubt to vex me at high noon.

THE STARRED COVERLET

A difficult achievement for true lovers
Is to lie mute, without embrace or kiss,
Without a rustle or a smothered sigh,
Basking each in the other's glory.

Let us not undervalue lips or arms
As reassurances of constancy,
Or speech as necessary communication
When troubled hearts go groping through the dusk;

Yet lovers who have learned this last refinement—
To lie apart, yet sleep and dream together
Motionless under their starred coverlet—
Crown love with wreaths of myrtle.

THE INTRUSION

Going confidently into the garden
Where she made much of you four hours ago
You find another person in her seat.

If your scalp crawls and your eyes prick at sight
Of her white motionless face and folded hands
Framed in such thunderclouds of sorrow,

Give her no word of consolation, man,
Dissemble your own anguish,
Withdraw in silence, gaze averted—
This is the dark edge of her double-axe:
Divine mourning for what cannot be.

PATIENCE

Almost I could prefer
A flare of anger
To your dumb signal of displeasure.

Must it be my task
To assume the mask
Of not desiring what I may not ask?

On a wide bed,
Both arms outspread,
I watch the spites do battle in my head,

Yet know this sickness
For stubborn weakness
Unconsonant with your tenderness.

O, to be patient
As you would have me patient:
Patient for a thousand nights, patient!

HAG-RIDDEN

I awoke in profuse sweat, arms aching,
Knees bruised and soles cut to the raw—
Preserved no memory of that night
But whipcracks and my own voice screaming.
Through what wild, flinty wastes of fury,
Hag of the Mill,
Did you ride your madman?

THE CURE

No lover ever found a cure for love
Except so cruel a thrust under the heart
(By her own hand delivered)
His wound was nine long years in healing
Purulent with dead hope,
And ached yet longer at the moon's changes . . .
More tolerable the infection than its cure.

TURN OF THE MOON

Never forget who brings the rain
In swarthy goatskin bags from a far sea:
It is the Moon as she turns, repairing
Damages of long drought and sunstroke.

Never count upon rain, never foretell it,
For no power can bring rain
Except the Moon as she turns; and who can rule her?

She is prone to delay the necessary floods,
Lest such a gift might become obligation,
A month, or two, or three; then suddenly
Not relenting but by way of whim
Will perhaps conjure from the cloudless west
A single rain-drop to surprise with hope
Each haggard, upturned face.

Were the Moon a Sun, we would count upon her
To bring rain seasonably as she turned;
Yet no one thinks to thank the regular Sun
For shining fierce in summer, mild in winter—
Why should the Moon so drudge?

But if one night she brings us, as she turns,
Soft, steady, even, copious rain
That harms no leaf nor flower, but gently falls
Hour after hour, sinking to the taproots,
And the sodden earth exhales at dawn
A long sigh scented with pure gratitude,
Such rain—the first rain of our lives, it seems,
Neither foretold, cajoled, nor counted on—
Is woman giving as she loves.

SELDOM, YET NOW

Seldom, yet now: the quality
Of this fierce love between us——
Seldom the encounter,
The presence always,
Free of oath or promise.

And if we were not so,
But birds of similar plumage caged
In the peace of everyday,
Could we still conjure wildfire up
From common earth, as now?

ANCHISES TO APHRODITE

Your sceptre awes me, Aphrodite,
  The knot-of-wisdom in your grasp.
Though you have deigned my couch to warm
  And my firm neck in love to clasp,

How am I more than a man-lion
  To you a goddess, the world's queen?
Ten thousand champions of your choice
  Are gone as if they had not been.

Yet while you grant me power to stem
  The tide's unalterable flow,
Enroyalled I await your pleasure
  And starve if you would have it so.

THE SECRET LAND

Every woman of true royalty owns
A secret land more real to her
Than this pale outer world:

At midnight when the house falls quiet
She lays aside needle or book
And visits there unseen.

Shutting her eyes, she improvises
A five-barred gate among tall birches,
Vaults over, takes possession.

Then runs, or flies, or mounts a horse
(A horse will canter up to greet her)
And travels where she will;

Can make grass grow, coax lilies up
From bud to blossom as she watches,
Lets fish eat from her palm;

Has founded villages, planted groves
And hollowed valleys for brooks running
Cool to a land-locked bay.

I never dared question my love
About the government of her queendom
Or its geography,

Nor followed her between those birches,
Setting one leg astride the gate,
Spying into the mist.

Yet she has pledged me, when I die,
A lodge beneath her private palace
In a level clearing of the wood
Where gentians grow with gillyflowers
And sometimes we may meet.

TO MYRTO OF MYRTLES

Goddess of Midsummer, how late
    You let me understand
My lines of head, life, fate
    And heart: a broad M brand
    Inerasable from either hand.

XII

TWO CHILDREN

You were as venturesome as I was shy:
Eager and inquisitive your eye.
    You set a nap on the plum, a haze on the rose,
And shooting stars across the wintry sky
    Flashed by in volleys for me when you chose.

None spoke with you, I alone worshipped you,
Child of the wave, child of the morning dew,
And in my dreams went chasing here and there
A fugitive beacon—your moon-yellow hair.

THE DANGEROUS GIFT

Were I to cut my hand
  On the sharp knife you gave me
  (That dangerous knife, your beauty),
I should know what to do:
  Bandage the wound myself
And hide the blood from you.

A murderous knife it is,
  As often you have warned me:
  For if I looked for pity
Or tried a wheedling note
  Either I must restore it
Or turn it on my throat.

TWICE OF THE SAME FEVER

No one can die twice of the same fever?
  Tell them it is untrue:
Have we not died three deaths, and three again,
  You of me, I of you?

The chill, the frantic pulse, brows burning,
  Lips broken by thirst—
Until, in darkness, a ghost grieves:
  'It was I died the first.'

Worse than such death, even, is resurrection.
  Do we dare laugh away
Disaster, and with a callous madrigal
  Salute the new day?

SURGICAL WARD: MEN

Something occurred after the operation
To scare the surgeons (though no fault of theirs)
Whose reassurance did not fool me long.
Beyond the shy, concerned faces of nurses
A single white-hot eye, focusing on me,
Forced sweat in rivers down from scalp to belly.
I whistled, gasped or sang, with blanching knuckles
Clutched at my bed-grip almost till it cracked:
Too proud, still, to let loose Bedlamite screeches
And bring the charge-nurse scuttling down the aisle
With morphia-needle levelled . . .
                                    Lady Morphia—
Her scorpion kiss and dark gyrating dreams—
She in mistrust of whom I dared out-dare,
Two minutes longer than seemed possible,
Pain, that unpurposed, matchless elemental
Stronger than fear or grief, stranger than love.

NIGHTFALL AT TWENTY THOUSAND FEET

A black wall from the east, toppling, arches the tall sky over
To drown what innocent pale western lights yet cover
Cloud banks of expired sunset; so good-bye, sweet day!
From earliest green you sprang, in green tenderly glide away . . .
Had I never noticed, on watch before at a humbler height,
That crowding through dawn's gate come night and dead of night?

THE SIMPLETON

To be defrauded often of large sums,
A whole year's income, even,
By friends trusted so long and perfectly
He never thought to ask receipts from them:
Such had been his misfortune.

He did not undervalue money, sighed for
Those banknotes, warm in the breast pocket,
For want of which his plans were baulked;
But could not claim that any man had left him
In complete poverty.

Easier to choke back resentment,
Never to sue them, never pit in court
His unsupported oath against theirs;
Easier not to change a forsworn friend
For a sworn enemy.

Easier, too, to scoff at legal safeguards,
Promissories on pale-blue foolscap
Sealed, signed, delivered before witnesses.
What legal safeguard had a full wallet
Carried among a crowd?

But though he preened himself on calmly
Cancelling irrecoverable debts,
It vexed him not to know
Why all his oldest, dearest friends conspired
To pluck him like a fowl.

THE WERE-MAN

Alone, alone and well alone at last,
Sentries by stealth outwitted, frontiers passed!
Yet walking alien thoroughfares you brood
Fearfully on the man by this feat rescued.

Never before, though trusted friends were few,
Though your own love of loves her oath outgrew,
Though off to the loud wars your children ran,
Never before closeted with a were-man.

Loathing his sylvan company, unable
To bed with him or set his place at table,
A savage life you lead, condemned to share
Your hearth with one whose habitat is nowhere.

THE PERSON FROM PORLOCK

... At that moment the Author was unfortunately called
out by a person on business from Porlock and on his return
found to his mortification that though he retained some vague
recollection of his vision, yet with the exception of eight or ten
scattered lines and images, all the rest had passed away.

Coleridge's preface to Kubla Khan: A Fragment

Unkind fate sent the Porlock person
To collect fivepence from a poet's house;
Pocketing which old debt he drove away,
Heedless and gay, homeward bound for Porlock.

O Porlock person, habitual scapegoat,
Should any masterpiece be marred or scotched,
I wish your burly fist on the front door
Had banged yet oftener in literature!

ESTABLISHED LOVERS

The established lovers of an elder generation
Dead from the waist down, every man of them,
Have now expired for sure
And, after nine days' public threnody,
Lapse to oblivion, or literature . . .
Clerks of Establishment must therefore search
For faces fit to people the blank spaces.

Faces enough are found, to pretend modesty
And mask their yearning for the public call:
Pluperfect candidates
Having long ceased to live as lovers do . . .
Clerks of Establishment, checking the dates,
Can feel no qualm in recommending Orders,
Titles and honorary love-doctorates.

Observe him well, the scarlet-robed academician
Stalled with his peers, an Order on his breast,
And (who could doubt it?) free
Of such despairs and voices as attended
His visits to the grotto below sea
Where once he served a glare-eyed Demoness
And swore her his unswerving verity.

THE QUIET GLADES OF EDEN

All such proclivities are tabulated—
By trained pathologists, in detail too—
The obscener parts of speech compulsively
Shrouded in Classic Latin.

But though my pleasure in your feet and hair
Is ungainsayable, let me protest,
(Dear love) I am no trichomaniac
And no foot-fetichist.

If it should please you, for your own best reasons,
To take and flog me with a rawhide whip,
I might (who knows?) surprisedly accept
This earnest of affection.

Nothing, agreed, is alien to love
When pure desire has overflowed it baulks,
But why must private sportiveness be viewed
Through public spectacles?

Enough, I will not claim a heart unfluttered
By these case-histories of aberrancy;
Nevertheless, a long cool draught of water
Or a long swim in the bay,

Serves to restore my wholesome appetite
For you and what we do at night together:
Which is no more than Adam did with Eve
In the quiet glades of Eden.

HERE LIVE YOUR LIFE OUT!

Window-gazing, at one time or another
In the course of travel, you must have startled at
Some coign of true felicity. 'Stay!' it beckoned,
'Here live your life out!' If you were simple-hearted
The village rose, perhaps, from a broad stream
Lined with alders and gold-flowering flags—
Hills, hay-fields, orchards, mills—and, plain to see,
The very house behind its mulberry-tree
Stood, by a miracle, untenanted!

Alas, you could not alight, found yourself jolted
Viciously on; public conveyances
Are not amenable to casual halts,
Except in sternly drawn emergencies—
Bandits, floods, landslides, earthquakes or the like—
Nor could you muster resolution enough
To shout: 'This is emergency, let me out!'
Rushing to grasp their brakes; so the whole scene
Withdrew forever. Once at the terminus
(As your internal mentor will have told you),
It would have been pure folly to engage
A private car, drive back, sue for possession.
Too far, too late:
Already bolder tenants were at the gate.

BURN IT!

Fetch your book here.
That you have fought with it for half a year
(Christmas till May)
Not intermittently but night and day
Need but enhance your satisfaction
In swift and wholesome action.

Write off the expense
Of stationery against experience,
And salvage no small beauties or half-lines.
You took the wrong turn, disregarded signs
Winking along your track,
Until too close-committed to turn back.

Fetch the book here
And burn it without fear,
Grateful at least that, having gone so far,
You still know what truth is and where you are,
With better things to say
In your own bold, unmarketable way.

JOAN AND DARBY

My friends are those who find agreement with me
In large measure, but not absolutely.
Little children, parasites and God
May flatter me with absolute agreement—
For no one lives more cynical than God.

As for my love, I gifted my heart to her
Twenty years ago, without proviso,
And in return she gifted hers to me;
Yet still they beat as two, unyielding in
Their honest, first reluctance to agree.

Other seasons, other thoughts and reasons,
Other fears or phases of the moon:
In lovingkindness we grow grey together—
Like Joan and Darby in their weather-lodge
Who never venture out in the same weather.

RUBY AND AMETHYST

Two women: one as good as bread,
  Bound to a sturdy husband.
Two women: one as rare as myrrh
  Bound only to herself.

Two women: one as good as bread,
  Faithful to every promise.
Two women: one as rare as myrrh,
  Who never pledges faith.

The one a flawless ruby wears
  But with such innocent pleasure
A stranger's eye might think it glass
  And take no closer look.

Two women: one as good as bread,
  The noblest of the city.
Two women: one as rare as myrrh,
  Who needs no public praise.

The pale rose-amethyst on her breast
  Has such a garden in it
Your eye could trespass there for hours,
  And wonder, and be lost.

About her head a swallow wheels
  Nor ever breaks the circuit:
Glory and awe of womanhood
  Still undeclared to man.

Two women: one as good as bread,
  Resistant to all weathers.
Two women: one as rare as myrrh,
  Her weather still her own.

SONG: COME, ENJOY YOUR SUNDAY!

Into your outstretched hands come pouring
Gifts by the cornucopiaful—
   What else is lacking?
Come, enjoy your Sunday
While yet you may!

Cease from unnecessary labours,
Saunter into the green world stretching far,
   Light a long cigar,
Come, enjoy your Sunday
While yet you may!

What more, what more? You fended off disaster
In a long war, never acknowledging
   Any man as master;
Come, enjoy your Sunday
While yet you may!

Are you afraid of death? But death is nothing:
The leaden seal set on a filled flask.
   If it be life you ask,
Come, enjoy your Sunday
While yet you may!

On a warm sand dune now, sprawling at ease
With little in mind, learn to despise the sea's
   Unhuman restlessness:
Come, enjoy your Sunday
While yet you may!

LEAVING THE REST UNSAID

Finis, apparent on an earlier page,
With fallen obelisk for colophon,
Must this be here repeated?

Death has been ruefully announced
And to die once is death enough,
Be sure, for any life-time.

Must the book end, as you would end it,
With testamentary appendices
And graveyard indices?

But no, I will not lay me down
To let your tearful music mar
The decent mystery of my progress.

So now, my solemn ones, leaving the rest unsaid,
Rising in air as on a gander's wing
At a careless comma,

INDEX OF FIRST LINES

353

354